C000057965

WHAT OTHERS ARE SAYING ABOUT SARAH THRIFT AND THIS BOOK

"The collaborative approach to strategy design that Sarah describes so articulately in her book is exactly what is needed to create real impact in the world."

- Zach Leverenz, CEO, EveryoneOn

"Sarah is a wonderful teacher and has transformed my ability to think strategically and communicate clearly. Whether you are reading *Designing a Strategy that Works* or attending her strategy courses, you are in for a life changing treat!"

- Janet Jenq, Internet Marketing Manager, eBay Inc.

"Sarah Thrift is one of the best problem solvers I have had the opportunity to work with."

- Jerome Rutler, Regional Chief Executive, Bureau Veritas

"No more wasted strategies! Sarah packs a punch with her insightful principles for creating a strategy that will work for your organization."

> – Stephanie Woo, Founder of Montessori on the Double and Author of *Raising Your Twins*

"Sarah offers pointed, direct solutions for constructing effective strategies, by looking at how things work in the real world, and building solutions based on these discovered realities. If you want to read a feel-good fluff piece about strategy, look elsewhere. If you want to actually understand how to construct effective strategy, look no further."

> – Daniel Cox, Manager, Business Customer Service, Sprint

"Working with Sarah enabled us to solve an important strategic question in a very cost-effective and pragmatic way."

> – Olivier Ropars, Marketing GM, eBay, Inc.

"If you are looking to take your organization in the right direction and increase both revenue and market share, start here."

> – Patrick Snow, International Best-Selling Author of *Creating Your Own Destiny*

"*With Designing A Strategy That Works* you will enhance your thinking and your communications, leading to better decisions and better results."

- Mark Bartosh, CPA, Director of Operations, Ms. Lam Montessori School

"An information-rich handbook for strategists and business users alike. A solid path to help strategize for one's business along with a good deal of detail to help consolidate understanding."

- Rosalind Rosewarne, Founder Rosewarne Gardens

"An incredibly insightful and useful book that explains how to harness individual skills in a team. After working with teams for years this book has taught me valuable lessons that have enhanced and enriched this experience."

- Janeclaire Stevens, Healthcare Manager

"*Designing a Strategy that Works* is an invaluable guide to creating the organization you want. Its practical, no-nonsense approach ensures you have at your fingertips the tools you need, to make the best decisions for your business."

- Tracey Stanton, Founder, Red Alchemy

DESIGNING A STRATEGY THAT WORKS

Defining Goals

Making Choices

Delivering Results

Sarah Thrift

AVIVA
PUBLISHING
NEW YORK

Designing A Strategy That Works:
Defining Goals, Making Choices, Delivering Results

Copyright © 2017 by Sarah Thrift. All rights reserved.

Published by:
Aviva Publishing
Lake Placid, NY
Office: +1 (518) 523-1320
www.AvivaPubs.com

All Rights Reserved. No part of this book may be used or reproduced
in any manner whatsoever without the expressed written permission
of the author. Address all inquiries to:

Insight Consultancy Solutions, Inc.
222 Broadway, 19th Floor, New York, NY 10001
Office: +1 (415) 413-8590
Email: info@insightconsults.com

ISBN: 978-1-9479371-1-6

Library of Congress: 2015909047

Editors: Irian Weber, Steve Hamilton
Cover/Book Illustrator: Tjaša Žurga Žabkar
Cover Layout: AnneMarie Ward
Book Layout: Steve Hamilton, Nishad Shamnadh, Elambaruthi Vimal
Author Photo: Ed Zappia

Every attempt has been made to properly source all quotes.

Printed in Great Britain

Third Edition, second printing

4 6 8 10 12 14

To my dear friend Irian,
whose wisdom, love and patience
is an inspiration

CONTENTS

INTRODUCTION

"Cat: Where are you going?
Alice: Which way should I go?
Cat: That depends on where you are going.
Alice: I don't know.
Cat: Then it doesn't matter which way you go."

Lewis Carroll, *Alice in Wonderland*

No organization can perform at its best unless everyone is moving in the same direction, towards the same goal. Yet only 14% of employees say they have a good understanding of their organization's direction and goal[1]. Like Alice, if an employee does not know their organization's direction and goal, then it does not really matter which direction they move in.

This is devastating: the talent and energy of nearly 9 out of 10 your employees are moving in random directions.

No one wants this. Yet it is sadly all too common, either as the result of a poorly communicated strategy, or for 35% of organizations, the result of no strategy at all.

Perhaps you are looking to design a new strategy for your organization, your team, or for a personal project. Or maybe you have been pursuing a specific strategy for a number of years and are wondering if it is time to craft a new strategy and to chart a fresh course. Maybe you previously developed a strategy but unexpected events in your market have you questioning whether your strategy is still valid.

Perhaps you have what, on paper, feels like a great strategy, but it never produces results. Or maybe you worked extensively with colleagues to generate support for your organization's new strategy only for too many colleagues to still behaving exactly as before. If so, you are far from alone.

Sixty-one percent of C-suite executives say their organization struggles to bridge the gap between strategy formulation and its day-to-day implementation[2].

I have been there. I know how frustrating it is not to have a clear direction, or to have a clear direction, but for colleagues to be pulling in different directions and pursuing everything but the agreed strategy. I have been on the receiving end of strategies that sounded good in theory but where no delivery plan had been developed nor even any practical pointers suggested. I don't enjoy being in these situations and I suspect you don't either.

Designing a Strategy that Works is a step-by-step guide to designing and implementing your strategy. By providing practical techniques and plenty of examples every step of the way, this book demystifies what strategy is and removes the sense of fear or resignation that can accompany the mere mention of the word.

By applying the tools, techniques and principles in this book, you will be able to shape the future of your organization. You will create clear goals that will enable you to make better choices. You will create goals which are shared, so everyone in your organization can move forward together. You will think deeply about how best to deliver your goals, and assess objectively the pros and cons of different options to do so. All this will prepare you to respond adeptly to unexpected events, including determining the implications of the event and as a result whether to stay or change course. You will also enhance your confidence about your strategy and your ability to deliver it—and that will shine through to colleagues, employees, investors and customers alike.

I have worked with hundreds of organizations all over the world, designing strategies and helping to implement them. I have worked with Fortune 500 companies and several of the largest NGOs. I have also worked with start-ups and with small founder-led nonprofits that are doing amazing work in the developing world. The techniques in this book have worked for all these organizations and I am delighted that by working through this book, these techniques can also work for you.

As a child, I happily spent hours solving math problems. This led me to study a Masters in Mathematics at Imperial College, London, where I graduated with first class honors and top of my class. I combined these skills with my passion for people, working as a strategy consultant at the world's preeminent management consultancy firm, McKinsey & Company.

My experience at McKinsey & Company was very formative—my first job out of college—and gave me the opportunity to learn from talented colleagues and clients. I used this experience as a policy advisor in the UK Treasury and before I was 30 ran a sales team of over 250 people.

In 2007, I created Insight Consultancy Solutions so I could design and deliver strategies for clients using the **actionable, rigorous** and **collaborative** principles described in this book. As a core philosophy, I also undertook to share and teach the techniques I used so that my clients would learn the skills to design their next strategy themselves.

In 2008, a client asked me if I could teach a course on these strategy techniques, promising to bring along other CEOs if I would teach the material. Since then, the demand for my course has grown and I have taught the course to hundreds of executives in Fortune 500 companies, NGOs and beyond.

Attendees of my courses repeatedly tell me that learning to think strategically and design a strategy has changed their lives. So often, they share how it has transformed their ability to structure their thinking, communicate ideas and make decisions. Working

3

with the hundreds of attendees has also changed my life, and it is thanks to my course participants, that this book has been possible.

Whether you are part of a multinational business or a one-person organization, whether your aim is for-profit or nonprofit, this book provides practical techniques to solve your most pressing problems, with tangible actions which deliver results. Use it as a reference, to be read and reread as you design and implement your strategy.

Throughout, I will be your partner for the change you want in your organization. Think of me as your coach and mentor, with you every step of the way. You don't need any specific experience to get started. All you need is a desire to deliver your goals and a willingness to try the techniques in this book.

I look forward to accompanying you on this exciting journey,

June 2017

FUNDAMENTALS

*"Failure comes only when we forget our ideals
and objectives and principles."*

Jawaharlal Nehru

KEY IDEAS

Strategy derives from the Greek word "στρατηγία" (strategia), meaning "the General's art". Whether you are a general, run a business, work in politics or lead a nonprofit organization, your fundamental tasks in designing your strategy remain the same: determining your goal, assessing your starting point, and once both of these are clearly determined, choosing the best set of actions to take you from your starting point to realizing your goal.

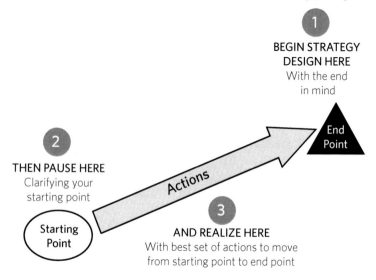

Figure 1: Clear starting and end points required to determine best actions

Great strategy starts with engaging your key stakeholders and reaching a shared view of your starting and end points. This may sound straightforward but there are likely to be many different views, both about where you are trying to get to and about where you are starting from. If you skip explicitly determining your starting and end points, you will never reach alignment on the set of actions to take.

A robust strategy emerges from exploring a comprehensive range of options and determining which can best deliver your goal. The process of thinking through and testing various options keeps you open to possibilities and forces an explicit weighing up of the different combinations and possibilities. In essence, this is about your ability to structure your thinking clearly and logically, to make decisions incisively and to translate abstract ideas into a plan that will work.

Being able to think in a structured way makes you a nimble navigator of your organization's destiny. If you have thought through your options, then as circumstances change you are able to respond quickly, thoughtfully and competitively. You will have already evaluated the strengths and weaknesses of your options and so won't need to go back to the drawing board every time there is a change.

A strong strategy creates a bridge from your starting point to your goal, where the bridge is made of a coherent set of deliverable actions. This means that your chosen actions work together and that were you were asked to deliver them, they are sufficiently tangible for you to do so.

A successful strategy is as explicit about the choices underpinning it as the choices that have been rejected. As Harvard Business School professor Michael Porter famously said, "The essence of strategy is choosing what not to do."[3] Success emerges from an explicit undertaking to stop any activities that are not part of the strategy. Whether your organization is big or small, a strategy that tries to do it all dilutes focus, overstretches resources and ultimately risks failure.

Any great strategist, like all the great generals of history, puts significant effort into ensuring that their choices are understood by all stakeholders, be they managers, employees, suppliers or customers. This is a crucial step in securing support from key people—your "army"—who you will need to deliver your strategy.

If your strategy is conceptually brilliant but its proposed actions are impractical or vague then you cannot expect it to be delivered, nor do you have the right to complain when it is not. Beware also of being seduced by a strategy that seems elegant but that it a bad fit for the culture of your organization. Any strategy which is a poor fit is doomed to disappear into your manager's desk drawer, never to be executed.

With a strategy grounded in the realism of your starting point, designed with strong input from the people who will need to deliver it and based on an objective assessment of all feasible options, you will have both the thinking and the support in place to succeed.

ACTIONABLE, RIGOROUS, COLLABORATIVE (ARC)

Actionable, **Rigorous** and **Collaborative**, or **ARC** for short, are the three principles that underpin my approach to strategy design and delivery. They are of such fundamental importance that I introduce them here, before describing the strategy process itself.

Actionable If you want to see your strategy delivered, it needs to be actionable—from the goal you set, to the choices you make to deliver the goal, to the delivery plan you create.

Rigorous Strategy is not rocket science. You don't need an MBA, a PhD, or experience working as a strategy consultant. What you do need is a rigorous approach to both the design and delivery of your strategy.

Collaborative Simple as it sounds, much of the best thinking is a result of getting the right people into the right discussions. Working collaboratively with key stakeholders throughout the strategy design process is one of the most critical ingredients for success. Being part of the discussions makes people more sympathetic to differing viewpoints and more likely to align behind an idea which is not their own. Remember to involve the people who will be delivering the strategy, they need to believe in it, so they can be ongoing advocates and have the vision and understanding to deliver it successfully.

Examples of being actionable include:
- Articulating a goal that is clear, stretching and sufficiently tangible for concrete actions to be determined.
- Ensuring every component of the research, and of the resulting strategy, can be translated into practical actions.
- Choosing a set of actions that can be easily created into a credible and realistic delivery plan.

If you are not rigorous, you risk missing out on opportunities or rubber-stamping an unvalidated strategy lurking in your mind. By being rigorous, you test what the best strategy really is. An overtly rigorous and objective approach will also be appreciated by stakeholders and helps build trust in your recommendations. Examples of being rigorous include:
- Precisely defining and articulating your goal.
- Being exhaustive about the range of possible options.
- Thoroughly exploring diverse sources of information and evidence.

To create collective ownership for design and delivery of the strategy, you need to be collaborative from the outset, starting with identifying key stakeholders. Then rigorously map how to engage your stakeholders throughout the process, for example by:
- Discussing and reaching alignment on the goal.
- Developing a shared view and diagnosis of the starting point.
- Collectively reviewing and discussing pros and cons of different options and making decisions from this shared understanding.

By collaboration I am not implying that you seek agreement on every point in the strategy—this risks watering everything down to the level where what is agreed isn't very meaningful. What I am talking about is alignment: everyone does not have to agree with every point, but everyone has been heard and is willing to align behind the collective viewpoints and decisions taken.

KEY CONCEPT: ALIGNMENT VS AGREEMENT[4]

Discussions often become challenging when each party believes they need to come to full agreement and get 100% of what they want.

Alignment is about having a shared understanding and commitment regarding a situation. It also means that once a decision is taken, every party is willing to support the decision as if it were their own.

By focusing on reaching alignment rather than agreement, the solution does not get stuck or watered down because everyone cannot fully agree. Working for alignment also creates focus on developing the best solution rather than what you want versus what I want.[5]

APPLYING ARC

While each principle is important in its own right, the real magic comes from applying ARC together.

Not only do plans need to be actionable, but so too does the list of evidence to gather.

You need to be just as rigorous in thinking through and setting up your framework for collaboration as you are with your evidence.

Collaboration isn't just about creating a shared goal but also about aligning on the level of rigor that will be sufficient to make decisions or collaborating to discuss if an option is sufficiently mapped out to be actionable.

ARC is the backbone of my approach to all strategy design and delivery work. If you make it part of your approach, you will give yourself the right foundations for a great strategy.

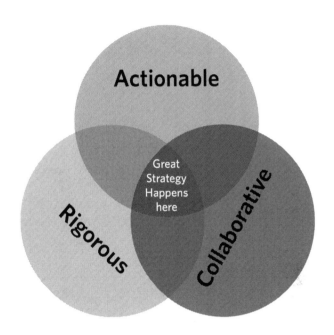

Figure 2: ARC, the three key principles

STRATEGY IN 5D

Strategy in 5D describes the five-step process I use to craft and implement a strategy that works. Its backbone is ARC and it uses tools and techniques that structure and test your thinking, which is the heart of what you need for a robust strategy.

Each step seeks to answer a specific question:
- **D_1efine:** What is your goal and end point?
- **D_2iagnose:** What is your current situation and starting point?
- **D_3evelop:** What are all the viable options to reach your goal?
- **D_4ecide:** What is the best set of options to reach your goal?
- **D_5eliver:** What is your plan to deliver?

Steps **D_1** to **D_4** relate to the design of the strategy and step **D_5** relates to delivery of the strategy[6]. The following tables lay this out, with Figure 3 providing a summary of concepts and deliverables which you can use and return to as a reference, as you work through the process.

Strategy in 5D		
Step	**Chapter**	**Actions**
D₁efine	1.1 Define Your Goal	Articulate goal as question ↓ Brainstorm sub-questions ↓
	1.2 Map Your Domain	Structure sub-questions
D₂iagnose	2.1 Diagnose Your Situation	Gather facts ↓ Draw insights ↓ Share findings
D₃evelop	3.1 Generate Hypotheses	Develop hypotheses ↓ Gather evidence
	3.2 Test Hypotheses	Repeat until hypotheses confirmed or disproved ↓ Draw insights ↓ Share findings
D₄ecide	4.1 Make Choices	Review combinations ↓ Debate scenarios ↓
	4.2 Write Your Strategy	Document choices
D₅eliver	5.1 Communicate Your Strategy	Communicate strategy ↓ Pilot approach ↓
	5.2 Deliver Results	Adapt approach ↓ Track progress
ARC at every step		

Figure 3: Strategy in 5D

Key Concepts	Deliverables
SMART ONE question CORD	D_1efine Question Frame
MECE (Mutually Exclusive, Collectively Exhaustive)	D_1efine Question Tree
Dummy deck One message per slide Cognitive biases: ASCOSCA (Ask Oscar!) SWOT and PESTLE The Minto Pyramid Principle®	D_2iagnosis Information Table D_2iagnosis Document
SMT (Specific, Measurable, Testable) hypotheses	D_3evelop Evidence Table
Estimates grid Summary versus Synthesis "So whats" 80:20 rule (Pareto's Law) Prioritization matrix	D_3evelop Findings Tables D_3evelop Conclusions Table
FLIRT (Financial, Limitations, Implementation, Risk Together) Storyline, Storyboard, ORCAS, TOADS	D_4ecide Table D_4ecide Document
WIN (What, Impact, Needs)	Strategy in 5D Document
Audience and their needs Desired outcomes	D_5eliver Launch Communications Plan
COST and ADAPT Governance and Delivery Office Piloting and Milestones	D_5elivery Workstreams Table D_5elivery Plan

CASE STUDY: ITC SOLUTIONS

To demonstrate the techniques, each chapter will include working examples for ITC Solutions, a fictitious IT company reselling products and providing services.

You will get to know ITC Solutions well as we apply the Strategy in 5D process to create its strategy.

ABOUT ITC SOLUTIONS

- ITC Solutions (ITC) is a technology provider with two core businesses: reselling IT products and provision of IT services.
- Over the past three years it has experienced 8% revenue growth, generating revenue of $360m in 2015.
- Profitability has been flat in this same period and in 2015 was $35m.
- ITC's recent corporate plan projected $42m profit for 2018, but this was rejected by the leadership team as insufficiently ambitious.
- The CEO believes the next two years (2016-2018) are critical in reinvigorating the company and requires reaching a $50m profit.
- Several large services contracts are up for renewal during the next two years (2016-2018).
- Growth of the business has been slowed down by lack of capabilities, such as IT skills to support both internal transformation and customer requirements.

GETTING STARTED

To get started with Strategy in 5D, and instill an actionable, rigorous and collaborative (ARC) approach, I recommend you:

1. **Appoint a strategy design leader.** This should be the person who steers the thinking and who holds overall responsibility for design of the strategy (steps D_1 to D_4 of Strategy in 5D). You will later need someone to oversee the delivery (step D_5), although this may not be the same person who heads up the design.
2. **Select a strategy design team.** The strategy design leader should form a team who will do the day-to-day work on the strategy design. Their role will include identifying and gathering information, drawing insights from the information, making recommendations on choices and preparing communications and presentations about the strategy.
3. **Confirm your objectives, at least for the design phase:** These are likely to be focused on the design of your strategy.
4. **List all decision makers and stakeholders:** A person's formal power, denoted by their role, is not necessarily the same as their informal power, so consider both as you determine which category each of your stakeholders sits in:
   - Who will actually make the decisions on the choices underpinning the strategy?
   - Who else has a stake in the outcome?
   - Who else has important influence?
5. **Create a steering committee** and schedule steering committee meetings. The steering committee should be formed from your key stakeholders. Their role is to provide regular input into the thinking and findings and also to be part of brainstorming meetings and crucial discussions about choices. I recommend that steering committee meetings are held at least once every two weeks for two hours, and if your committee has time, weekly, with the understanding that until you reach the final strategy, all prior steering committee meetings are working sessions and not formal presentations.

6. **Determine length of strategy design process (steps D_1 to D_4):** I recommend that you allow yourself between 10 and 14 weeks to develop your strategy. In my experience it doesn't help to take any longer. Decisions that are hard after 10 weeks are still going to be just as hard after 18 weeks. If you need to go faster, you may be able to complete the strategy design in eight weeks, but I doubt it can be done faster if you want to be sufficiently rigorous and thoughtful in gathering information and have time to reflect on what it means. Busy calendars can make the time commitment a concern. There is no easy solution to this, but deftly done, it can help to remind stakeholders that your strategy is your destiny and so it really pays to invest the time to get it right.

7. **Schedule strategy design team time:** Ensure regular formal time for the team to work together, including full discussion of findings.

8. **Document your Terms Of Reference (TOR):** This should cover the strategy design phase and detail the objectives, roles, stakeholders and timings (points 3 to 7 above). The TOR ensures that the strategy design team and stakeholders all have a clear and shared understanding of their role. Ideally the TOR is created collaboratively by the strategy design team.

9. **Get buy-in from all key stakeholders.** Start with taking them through and seeking alignment on the TOR. Do not forget to remind them of the role you want them to play, e.g. whether on the steering committee, and the time required from them to design an effective strategy.

An example TOR for ITC is provided opposite.

TERMS OF REFERENCE: EXAMPLE FOR ITC

Objective: To collaboratively develop a rigorous and actionable strategy to maximize ITC's success.

Approach: Use the tools and process from *Designing A Strategy That Works.*

Decision makers:
- Jackie Johnson, CEO
- Annette Spillars, CFO
- Jim Vaughan, COO

Key stakeholders:
- Raghu Jain, Head of Large Business
- Penny Barnes, Head of Small and Medium Business (SMB)
- Desmond Evans, Head of Product Business
- Lisa Evereau, Head of Services Business

Other stakeholders:
- All staff
- Customers
- Suppliers

Strategy design leader:
- Jim Vaughan, COO

Strategy design team:
- James Edwards, Commercial Manager
- Saffron Jones, Sales Executive, Large Business
- Jennifer Jackson, Marketing Manager, SMB
- Tyler Adams, Product Manager, Product Business
- Lydia Dyson, Services Manager, Services Business

Timeframe:

12 weeks

Strategy design team schedule:
The strategy design team will meet every Tuesday at 8.30am for a five-hour working session, with lunch provided. In addition, each team member is expected to devote approximately one day a week to work on the step currently underway.

Steering committee members:
- Jackie Johnson, CEO
- Annette Spillars, CFO
- Raghu Jain, Head of Large Business
- Penny Barnes, Head of SMB
- Desmond Evans, Head of Product Business
- Lisa Evereau, Head of Services Business

Steering committee role:
Provide guidance, insight and encouragement to the strategy design team as they craft the strategy and plan. Supportively challenge the strategy design team to get to the best answer. Reinforce the importance and value of ARC, and of the Strategy in 5D process, as a way of working.

Steering committee schedule:
Steering committee will meet eight times, two hours per meeting except for the final meeting of three hours. Meetings will take place approximately once every two weeks. Strategy design team will share information, findings and ideas for discussion, and as the thinking develops, will test the emerging strategy.

STEERING COMMITTEE MEETING SCHEDULE	
D_1efine	Meeting 1 • Review TOR, D_1efine Question Frame and D_1efine Question Tree
D_2iagnose	Meeting 2 • Review D_2iagnosis of current situation • Determine any further information required • Discuss implications of the D_2iagnosis for potential solutions available
D_3evelop	Meeting 3 • Hear list of hypotheses to be tested • Provide feedback on any suggested changes or additions to hypotheses • Review proposed evidence and provide ideas for additional evidence and sources Meetings 4, 5 and 6 • Hear latest findings on the hypotheses • Determine what required to prove or disprove remaining hypotheses
D_4ecide	Meeting 7 • Discuss recommended choices • If there are big strategic choices to be made, ensure full discussion • Reach alignment on the key choices Meeting 8 • Hear final presentation of strategy and high-level implementation plan • Provide feedback for any changes and guidance on how to execute
D_5eliver	Meetings to be determined once strategy finalized

You are now ready to embark on the first step **D_1efine**.

D$_1$efine

D$_2$iagnose

D$_3$evelop

D$_4$ecide

D$_5$eliver

1.1

DEFINE YOUR GOAL

*"It isn't that they can't see the solution.
It is that they can't see the problem."*

G. K. Chesterton

Strategy in 5D

Step	Chapter	Actions
D₁efine	1.1 Define Your Goal	Articulate goal as question ↓ Brainstorm sub-questions ↓
	1.2 Map Your Domain	Structure sub-questions
D₂iagnose	2.1 Diagnose Your Situation	Gather facts ↓ Draw insights ↓ Share findings
D₃evelop	3.1 Generate Hypotheses	Develop hypotheses ↓ Gather evidence ←
	3.2 Test Hypotheses	Repeat until hypotheses confirmed or disproved ↓ Draw insights ↓ Share findings
D₄ecide	4.1 Make Choices	Review combinations ↓ Debate scenarios ↓
	4.2 Write Your Strategy	Document choices
D₅eliver	5.1 Communicate Your Strategy	Communicate strategy ↓ Pilot approach ↓
	5.2 Deliver Results	Adapt approach ↓ Track progress

ARC at every step

KEY IDEAS

You cannot design an effective strategy—that is choose a set of actions that will be effective—if you are not clear on what these actions are supposed to achieve, that is, your goal. Simply put, there can be no ambiguity in what your goal is.

A well-formulated goal should adhere to the ARC principles introduced in the previous chapter, Fundamentals. This means that the goal and resulting end point should be actionable, rigorously thought-through and determined collaboratively.

Questions stimulate thinking and discovery, so it works best to express your goal as a question. Take time to try different questions that express different goals or that emphasize different aspects of a particular goal. Ensure you rigorously commit every possible question to paper, with precise wording, so no question is missed, assumed or left ambiguous.

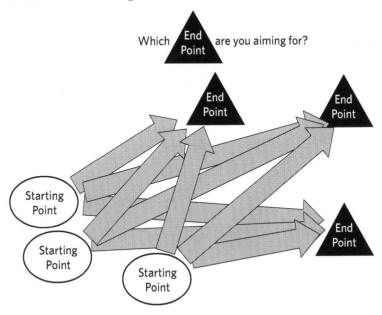

Figure 4: Need clear end point to determine right actions and path

You want your question to be stretching while remaining actionable. If it becomes watered down, you may later miss potential solutions.

Keep going until your question precisely expresses what you want. You can often feel instinctively if this is the case. The emphasis on the right question might sound black and white and that's because it is. There is most often only one formulation that is precisely right and since your entire strategy will be developed to answer this question, you need to get it right. As author Stephen R. Covey says, "If your ladder is not leaning against the right wall, every step you take gets you to the wrong place faster."[7]

Once you have your question, be sure to frame it by including context to the question and by listing the result you want from the question. This minimizes the risk of the question being misunderstood.

To check the precision of your question and its framing, and to ensure buy-in, involve your stakeholders in its formulation. Don't be surprised if there are diverse views about what the question should be. Make sure everyone is heard and ideally ask a person outside of the process to facilitate the discussion, with the aim of reaching alignment behind one question.

As I say when teaching my strategy courses, your question shapes your destiny, so take the time to get it right.

DELIVERABLES, CONCEPTS, ARC AND MEETINGS

Below is the relevant except of the Strategy in 5D key concepts and deliverables table from page 15. The terms covered here will be expanded on during the chapter. You'll also find a similar table in all subsequent chapters.

Step	Chapter	Key Concepts	Deliverables
D_1efine	1.1 Define Your Goal	SMART ONE question CORD	D_1efine Question Frame

Examples of applying ARC for defining your goal:

- Your goal and question are stretching, yet **actionable**.
- Your question is worded precisely and with **rigor**.
- Your question is developed through a **collaborative** process.

The key meetings required to complete this chapter are:

- Strategy design team:
  - Determine question
  - Complete D_1efine Question Frame (may require two meetings)
- Steering committee:
  - Review D_1efine Question Frame
  - Strategy design team may want to meet stakeholders individually prior to meeting together

GETTING CLEAR ON YOUR GOAL

Why are you embarking on a strategy design process? Are you looking to grow your overall business or a particular part of it? Are you looking for new areas where you can successfully operate? Do you have a target to meet and need to determine the best actions to deliver it? Is there a particular obstacle to meeting this year's targets and you need to decide on the best actions to tackle it? Have you determined that you have a strong product offering but sales and business development are letting you down? Or is there something bugging you that you know you need to fix to support better results, but you are not sure how best to fix it? All of these examples—and we could go on—are goals that can be addressed through Strategy in 5D.

There are several considerations when determining your goal. One is your role in the organization: this impacts the level of the goal you can set, as you need a mandate for setting and delivering your goal. If you are the CEO, then the full strategy of the organization is within your mandate. If you are responsible for marketing in one of the organization's divisions, then your goal needs to be related to these responsibilities.

A second consideration is that you do not want to be running multiple goals through the Strategy in 5D process simultaneously. Focus your time and energy on one goal which you thoroughly apply the Strategy in 5D techniques to. Later, over the coming months and years, you can apply the same Strategy in 5D process to other goals, but right now more than one goal would be counterproductive.

A third consideration is striking a balance between boldness and pragmatism. If you try to solve everything with an overarching goal that is too nebulous, you are setting yourself up for failure. At the same time, if the actions required to deliver your goal do not require deep thinking, then no need to apply Strategy in 5D.

What is the one goal to which you will apply Strategy in 5D this time around? Why are you reading this book? What will have the most impact if you address it? Jot down your thoughts below. You may want to try visualizing your end goal as you do this. If there a few different possibilities, write these down and over the next couple of days keep returning to your list until you can get clarity on your goal:

As we know from ARC, your goal should not be determined in a vacuum, so be collaborative. Talk to stakeholders and to the strategy design team. You do not need a word-perfect goal since we will rewrite the goal as a very precise question as part of the Strategy in 5D process, but you do need enough clarity to be sure you are all referring to the same goal.

EXPRESSING YOUR GOAL AS A QUESTION

To consider what makes a good question let's start with a few examples of goals expressed as questions.

Given what you read about ITC in "About ITC Solutions" on page 16 and thinking about what an appropriate goal would be, how fitting are the following questions for ITC? As you read through, remember that your question frames your entire strategy.

1. What makes ITC profitable?

2. Can ITC double its business?

3. What organizational changes are required for ITC to deliver $50m profit?

4. What actions can ITC best take to achieve sustainable profit of at least $50m per year from 2018?

_____

_____

_____

_____

_____

5. Create a proposition to generate significant and sustainable return for ITC and the customer.

_____

_____

_____

_____

_____

6. How can ITC add 50% to its revenue in the next two years, while at least maintaining current profit margins?

_____

_____

_____

_____

_____

We will return to these questions shortly.

MAKING YOUR QUESTION A SMART ONE

A great question is a **SMART ONE**. You're probably familiar with the SMART acronym which defines effective objectives as being Specific, Measurable, Actionable, Relevant and Time-bound. To this, I add ONE, which stands for Open, Non-assumptive and Expansive. Check your question to see if it is a SMART ONE:

Specific Is articulated without ambiguity. Ever word matters, so be exact to express your intent precisely.

Measurable Contains components that can be used to assess success, for example a profit target or measure of social impact.

Actionable Gives rise to concrete actions that ultimately realize the goal.

Relevant Gets to the heart of what is most important.

Time-bound Provides a time-frame during which the answer to the question—the strategy—must be delivered.

Open Is an open question, that is, it cannot be answered with a yes or no.

Non-assumptive Does not contain any implicit assumptions about the solution nor preclude any possible solutions.

Expansive Has the same scope as the goal, giving space for a comprehensive range of viable options in response. Apply Einstein's advice: "Everything should be as simple as it can be but not simpler."[8]

EXERCISE: IDENTIFYING SMART ONE QUESTIONS

Let's return to the six possible questions for ITC. Consider how each question performs against each of the SMART ONE criteria:

Answer Yes / No	S	M	A	R	T	O	N	E
1. What makes ITC profitable?								
2. Can ITC double its business?								
3. What organizational changes are required for ITC to deliver $50m profit?								
4. What actions can ITC best take to achieve sustainable profit of at least $50m per year from 2018?								
5. Create a proposition to generate significant and sustainable return for ITC and the customer.								
6. How can ITC add 50% to its revenue in the next two years, while at least maintaining current profit margins?								

Commentary on the above table can be found in the Appendix, on page 313.

TESTING THE EXPANSIVENESS OF YOUR QUESTION

A helpful way to test if your question is the right one, with the appropriate level of expansiveness, and addresses the goal, is to ask: "What are the questions behind the question, and which question are you really seeking to answer?"

Let's consider the following question:

> What changes could be made to pricing to reach $50m profitability in 2018?

A question behind this question is:

> What offerings are needed to best deliver $50m profit in 2018?

We can repeat the same step again, seeking a question behind this question:

> What actions can be taken to deliver $50m profit in 2018?

Then decide which question provides the most appropriate scope for your strategy. To come to the conclusion that the first question is the right question, you would need to have done prior work and already have determined that a focus on pricing would generate all viable options for reaching $50m in 2018.

Working through this for ITC to ensure the question is a SMART ONE, and knowing the context about growth having been slowed down by lack of capabilities, then a suitable question is:

> What actions can ITC best take to develop capabilities and achieve sustainable profit of at least $50m per year from 2018?

GETTING TO THE RIGHT QUESTION

Crafting a SMART ONE question in collaboration with your stakeholders is an excellent way to create buy-in and ensure you get to the right question. The best way to do this is to get all key stakeholders around the table, or at least on a conference call.

From there either brainstorm potential questions from a blank sheet of paper or review a shortlist of potential questions. With either approach, make sure that everyone's views on potential questions are heard. This works best if someone who is not a stakeholder facilitates the discussion, engaging everyone and ensuring that all views are heard impartially.

Pay attention to the specific words each person uses. Nuances are important. Seemingly small changes in the wording of the question can cause big changes in the direction the strategy takes.

As the discussion progresses it's important that everyone can see and compare all proposed formulations of the question. Write down all suggestions, with exact wording, on a whiteboard or flipchart.

Be open to differences of opinion and work through them. Often it's these differences that really open up the discussion and allow the question to evolve into a much better one. Differences of opinion or variations in focus, whether subtle or not, need to be understood if the subsequent strategy is to be successful.

Reread and rewrite the question until everyone is comfortable. If you get stuck, take a break and come back to it. There really is only one question that is better than any other and you can usually feel whether you have got to it.

By spending time to get the question right in the first place it's extremely rare that you need to change it later. Bear in mind the strategy design process is at most four months long, so changes to the question would only be those dictated by significant changes in external circumstances—such as a change in regulation—that occur during that time. In all my years of consulting, I cannot think of one instance where a change was needed.

Remember, your aim is alignment. You don't need every stakeholder to agree with every word. You only need them to feel sufficiently comfortable to align with it. If you aim for 100% agreement on every word, you risk diluting the question through too many compromises.

KEY CONCEPT: GOOD MEETING PRACTICE

For every meeting, whether it's a one-off or routine, think about what you want the outcome to be and how you can best achieve it. Not only does this help you get what you want, but participants will be happier if you make good use of their time.

Prior to the meeting:
- **Desired outcomes:** Write these down, including any decisions that need to be made and how you want attendees to feel as a result of the meeting.

- **Clear agenda:** Identify the items you want to cover and the time allocated to each. You may want to do this by consulting participants. Then circulate the agenda to all participants.

- **Meeting approach:** Determine the nature of the meeting. For each item will there be a question to discuss, slides presented, a brainstorm or something else?

- **Pre-read:** Be sure to circulate any materials with time for attendees to read in advance. Highlight any topics or questions to think about prior to the meeting.

- **Delineated roles:** Ensure you know in advance who will play what role, including who will chair or facilitate the meeting.

During the meeting:
- **Frame the meeting:** Even if you think it's obvious, remind participants of the purpose of the meeting and the role you want them to play (e.g. provide feedback, make a decision, debate implications). This need only take a couple of minutes and is invaluable for getting all participants to a common starting point.

- **Set ground rules:** Discuss the behaviors required to ensure success upfront. You don't need to do this in every meeting, just with a new group or if there's an issue with an existing group, e.g. to agree no cell phones during the meeting.

- **Recap previous meeting:** Participants may not remember the detail of the previous meeting. A recap can quickly address this, with two or three slides that refresh memories without reopening the previous agreements. Include sign-off of the last meeting's minutes.

- **Take minutes:** Give an attendee responsibility for writing the minutes. Emphasize the importance of the minutes being accurate and comprehensive. If they are selective, you will lose trust.

- **Stay on track:** Start on time and then manage time so you get through the agenda. If further discussion is required, set up a separate time.

- **Maintain roles:** Do not deviate from roles decided for the meeting. For example, if your role is to facilitate, do not start offering your views.

- **Articulate clear next steps:** Wrap up each item with clear actions with owners and timing for each.

- **Next meeting:** Agree next meeting as required, with date, time, location and purpose.

After the meeting:
- **Circulate minutes:** Include actions, owners and timing within 48 hours of meeting.

- **Review minutes:** To ensure accountability, review the minutes and actions at the beginning of the next meeting.

CLIENT EXAMPLE: THE RIGHT QUESTION

I was sitting around the table with four stakeholders of a large multinational company working in travel and entertainment. One of the stakeholders described what he believed the question to be: reviewing an existing business, to ensure we had the best commercial model.

It soon became apparent, however, that the other three stakeholders each had different views on the key question.

Another stakeholder wanted to review the whole industry and from there create the commercial model, not just for the existing business, but for all future businesses.

The stakeholders were very surprised that each had such a different view on the question. A fantastic debate ensued and a more fitting question than any of the previous four emerged.

Through this process the stakeholders also realized they had unknowingly been holding different objectives and expectations and that a simple meeting got these resolved and in so doing removed previously unseen obstacles to success.

The stakeholders thanked me for helping them reach an aligned position. This hadn't been my direct objective—which had been to get to the right question—and yet it was invaluable to get this alignment, and also the engagement between stakeholders, which continued throughout the project and beyond.

FRAMING YOUR QUESTION WITH CORD

Once you have written your question as a SMART ONE, add framing to ensure that it is understood with the appropriate context. If your organization has a template it uses to frame questions and problems then it may make sense to use it here.

The framing I use includes context to your question and comments on the opportunity and scope of the question. I also include any further details on the desired results from answering the question and the deliverables from the strategy design process. Collectively these form the acronym CORD:

Context The background information you would tell someone to give them sufficient context on the question.

Opportunity Any stipulations or constraints to the scope that are not articulated in the question. For example, a question may only be applicable to certain geographies or business units.

Results Any results that need to be achieved beyond those explicitly articulated in the question. For example, non-financial objectives such as industry accreditations or levels of employee retention.

Deliverables What you want to come out of the strategy design work. This could include a written strategy document, business plan, interim milestones, resource plan, technology plan, governance plan and a comms plan.

I combine both the SMART ONE question and the CORD into the D$_1$efine Question Frame, as per the example for ITC overleaf:

D₁EFINE QUESTION FRAME	
SMART ONE Question	What actions can ITC best take to develop capabilities and achieve sustainable profit of at least $50m per year from 2018?[9]
Context	<ul><li>ITC is a technology provider with two core businesses: reselling of IT products and provision of IT services</li><li>Over the past three years, ITC has experienced 8% revenue growth, yielding $360m in 2015</li><li>Profitability has been flat in this same period and in 2015 was $35m</li><li>A corporate plan estimated $42m profit for 2018, but this was rejected by the leadership team as insufficiently ambitious</li><li>The CEO believes the next two years are critical to reinvigorating the company and require reaching $50m profit</li><li>Several large services contracts are up for renewal during 2016-2018</li><li>Growth of the business has been slowed down by lack of capabilities, such as IT skills to support both internal and customer transformation</li></ul>
Opportunity	<ul><li>All business divisions, North America and Europe</li><li>Would consider new geographical markets as part of growth strategy</li></ul>

D₁EFINE QUESTION FRAME	
Results	• Profit in 2016 and 2017 needs to be at least $42m and $45m respectively • Establishment of a learning culture that encourages the testing of new initiatives and learning quickly what works and what does not

Deliverables	• A clear set of actions, that will be executed to deliver the strategy, including:
	  – Revenue and number of new customers as well as profit targets
	  – Description of new markets and new services provided and how to win new business in these
	  – The resources and capabilities that will be needed
	  – Governance of these actions including assigned owners for each set of actions and an approach to quickly pilot these
	  – Quarterly milestones for 2016, six-monthly for 2017 and 2018
	• Identification of risks and counter-measures
	• Communications approach to engage all members of business with this strategy

Figure 5: Example D₁efine Question Frame for ITC

Be sure not to skip completing the D_1efine Question Frame. It provides a consistent basis for work with all stakeholders. You can use your D_1efine Question Frame alongside your TOR to provide details of the process, your stakeholders and your question.

As you get immersed in the research and options, it is all too easy to lose sight of your goal and get lost in the weeds. To ensure I keep on track, I review both the TOR and the D_1efine Question Frame at least once a week during steps **D_1** to **D_4**. They bring you back to the whole picture, and in so doing, help ensure that you come up with a robust strategy that truely answers your question.

D_1EFINE QUESTION FRAME CHECKLIST

- Your question is a SMART ONE.
- Your question is written down.
- A question frame has been completed.
- Key stakeholders have been engaged in reviewing and ideally also in developing the question.
- Key stakeholders are in alignment with the question.
- Key stakeholders are aligned on the question frame, including each aspect of the CORD.

1.2

MAP YOUR DOMAIN

"Do not worry if you have built your castles in the air. They are where they should be. Now put the foundations under them."

Henry David Thoreau

Strategy in 5D		
Step	**Chapter**	**Actions**
D₁efine	1.1 Define Your Goal	Articulate goal as question ↓ **Brainstorm sub-questions**
	1.2 Map Your Domain	**Structure sub-questions**
D₂iagnose	2.1 Diagnose Your Situation	Gather facts ↓ Draw insights ↓ Share findings
D₃evelop	3.1 Generate Hypotheses	Develop hypotheses ↓ Gather evidence
	3.2 Test Hypotheses	Repeat until hypotheses confirmed or disproved Draw insights ↓ Share findings
D₄ecide	4.1 Make Choices	Review combinations ↓ Debate scenarios
	4.2 Write Your Strategy	Document choices
D₅eliver	5.1 Communicate Your Strategy	Communicate strategy ↓ Pilot approach
	5.2 Deliver Results	Adapt approach ↓ Track progress
ARC at every step		

KEY IDEAS

With your question defined, your next task is to identify sub-questions, that is, the questions you need to answer in order to answer your overall question. By breaking down the overall question into sub-questions, you create structure: a map of the domain you are operating in with the questions you need to answer in order to address your overall question.

Compare this for a moment with trying to directly answer your overall question without putting any further structure in place: it's a bit like starting an essay without having thought through any structure for your argument. It's hard to assess where best to start and it's all too easy to forget to include key points. Similarly, if you go straight to answering your overall question, there is a significant risk of missing potential solutions.

To be able to see new perspectives, you need to identify all possible sub-questions. This opens the door to unexpected insights, a greater range of solutions and in turn, a more robust strategy. Even if you have a hunch that a particular sub-question will not lead to a viable solution, still include it. Now is not the time to restrict thinking, it is the time to embrace all possibilities.

To avoid overlap, you want the sub-questions to either be completely distinct from one another or to be sub-questions of a sub-question, i.e. they break the sub-question down to the next level. This ensures you won't miss out on a potential line of investigation.

It helps to organize your sub-questions visually into a D_1efine Question Tree as depicted in Figure 6. The D_1efine Question Tree positions sub-questions relative to each other based on their content. Sub-questions become more detailed as you move to the right. The first tier of sub-questions are not too detailed and together they answer the overall question to their left. The next tier of questions to the right, tier two, are the sub-questions of the tier one sub-questions, and so on. In this way, the tree provides a structure to your thinking, making the relationship between the sub-questions explicit.

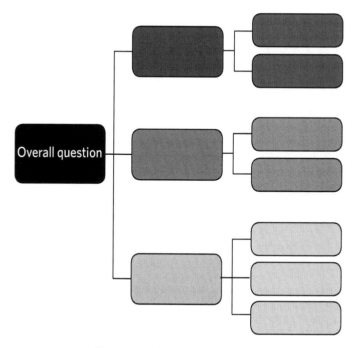

Figure 6: D₁efine Question Tree structure

You want as many tiers on your tree for the sub-questions of the final tier to be answerable without being broken down further.

Some sub-questions may be answered directly with facts, such as the majority of sub-questions relating to the past and present. Other sub-questions, such as those relating to future or potential opportunities cannot be answered by facts alone and will need to be answered with a combination of evidence, such as customer feedback and insights from experts. Such sub-questions can best be addressed through first generating hypotheses of the most plausible answers. Then, using the evidence you gather, each hypothesis can be tested, revised and ultimately confirmed or rejected. We will return to generating and testing hypotheses in much more depth in chapters 3.1 and 3.2.

As with every step of Strategy in 5D, be sure to get alignment from your key stakeholders. This means getting buy-in for your D₁efine Question Tree. That way, you can be sure that the map of the domain it provides does not miss anything important. You also safeguard against stakeholders coming back at a later stage and asking why a certain question or set of questions were not considered.

DELIVERABLES, CONCEPTS, ARC AND MEETINGS

Step	Chapter	Key Concepts	Deliverables
D₁efine	1.2 Map your Domain	MECE (Mutually Exclusive, Collectively Exhaustive)	D₁efine Question Tree

Examples of application of ARC for mapping your domain are:

- Sub-questions are **actionable**: either they can be answered as is, or are broken down into further sub-questions, until every sub-question of the furthest right tier is answerable as is.
- Sub-questions are generated with **rigor** to ensure that nothing is missed.
- Key stakeholders review and align with the D₁efine Question Tree and where possible, are also engaged **collaboratively** in the generation of sub-questions.

The key meetings required to complete this chapter are:

- Strategy design team:
  - Brainstorm sub-questions and the organize them into a D₁efine Question Tree
- Steering committee:
  - Review D₁efine Question Tree and make any changes until reach alignment on the tree

BREAKING YOUR QUESTION INTO SUB-QUESTIONS

Sub-questions break open the overall question into logical and more manageable components. You can break down all sorts of questions—not just strategy ones. One of my colleagues at McKinsey & Company used to map out a question tree to determine options for her Friday night out!

Most sub-questions begin with either "what" or "how" and all need to be formulated as a question, not a statement. Every sub-question needs to be complete in and of itself—although it may still require further breaking down to a level where it can be practically analyzed or researched.

Earlier we covered the idea of the overall question being right. There is no one right set of sub-questions, although you can have a wrong set if there are gaps or overlaps. To check this, confirm that by answering all the sub-questions, you answer your overall question, without the need for any further sub-questions.

Let's take a couple of examples:

Question 1: What is the most time- and cost- efficient way to get from New York City to Washington D.C. leaving tomorrow morning and arriving by 2pm?

Sub-questions could be:
1.1. What are all the ways to get from New York City tomorrow morning to Washington D.C. by 2pm?
1.2. How much does each of these cost?
1.3. How much time does each of these take?

Question 2: In the next 12 months, how can Generate, a youth nonprofit, increase impact for its users without increasing costs?

Sub-questions here could be:
2.1. How does Generate define and measure impact today?
2.2. Is this sufficient as a definition and measure of impact, and if not, what changes are needed?
2.3. What levers does Generate have to increase impact without increasing overall costs?

2.4. How easy are the levers to implement and show results within the next 12 months?

2.5. Given the above questions, what actions should Generate take and what is the plan to do this?

Examples of more detailed sub-questions that would sit under sub-question 1.1 are:

1.1.1. Which airlines fly from New York City to Washington D.C. tomorrow morning that arrive by 2pm?

1.1.2. What are the flight times?

1.1.3. Which of these flights have remaining seats?

While sub-questions can feed into another sub-question, no sub-question should directly overlap another sub-question, so unless a sub-question adds something new, it should be eliminated.

Let's suppose that for question 1, we also asked the following tier one sub-question:

What are the cheapest options of traveling between New York City and Washington D.C. tomorrow morning by 2pm?

Review this sub-question alongside sub-questions 1.1 to 1.3. Does it overlap? Yes. It overlaps with sub-questions 1.1 and 1.2.

Does it add anything new? No. To avoid overlaps, either eliminate 1.4 and use 1.1 and 1.2, or replace 1.1 and 1.2 with 1.4.

Let's return to questions 1.1.1 to 1.1.3. Do these overlap with questions 1.1 to 1.3? Yes, they overlap with question 1.1. Do they add anything? Yes, since they provide structure to what needs to be considered when answering sub-question 1.1. Which means unlike question 1.4, we don't want to just delete them. We will need them later when we structure our questions into a Define Question Tree.

GENERATING SUB-QUESTIONS

A great approach for generating your sub-questions is for the strategy design team to brainstorm them. If you have stakeholders who are willing to roll up their sleeves, involve them in the brainstorming too.

It works well to ask attendees to think in advance what the sub-questions could be. If you are facilitating the meeting, you may want to brainstorm your own list of sub-questions prior to the meeting and be ready to check against this list towards the end of the meeting once everyone has had the opportunity to share their sub-questions.

Do not limit your thinking too early. The only way to make sure you generate all relevant sub-questions is to first come up with all possible questions you might want to answer, in order to answer your overall question. So allow space for the seemingly irrelevant questions as the best solution can often come from places we least expect.

A good approach is to ask everyone to write their sub-questions on large Post-it® notes. That way everybody can share their sub-questions by placing Post-it® notes on whiteboards or walls, and later when structuring the sub-questions into a D$_i$efine Question Tree, you can easily move them around.

I highly recommend you read each of your sub-questions out loud, as this brings additional clarification and crystallization, beyond what can be achieved by just sounding them each out in your head. It often leads to a refinement of the wording of each sub-question and stimulates new sub-questions.

Check that the questions are not closed (answerable by yes or no) and are articulated in a way that allows a range of possible solutions and does not lead to a particular answer to the exclusion of others.

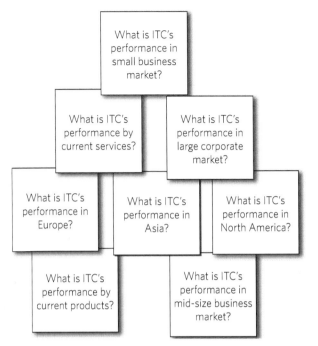

Figure 7: Example Post-it® notes from sub-question brainstorm

Make your sub-questions as concise as possible without losing meaning. Be sure that they are all expressed as questions, not thoughts, ramblings or answers. There is no limit to the number of sub-questions. Just confirm that as well as more high-level sub-questions, you also have sub-questions that are not too big to be addressed as is. If any sub-questions require further breaking down and there are no sub-questions that do this, then you are missing sub-questions.

Do not despair if you find yourself in a sea of sub-questions that seems overwhelming. Having a lot of sub-questions is in fact a good sign that you are not missing anything.

When you feel that you have most of the sub-questions, begin grouping them by topic. There is no single way to group sub-questions, often the grouping that makes most sense is the one that is in line with how information is available. For example, you might group sub-questions about the internal situation and performance of the organization together, or put those about customer needs together, or those about regulation together.

You may need to make a choice between different groups to avoid overlaps, especially as you look at more detailed sub-questions. For example, if you have sub-questions about financial performance, one way to group these might be around geographies, that is financial performance in the different geographies today and, if your scope permits, the potential financial performance in new geographies. Another way could be by customer segment, for example, grouping the sub-questions by customer size (large, medium, small business and consumer). A further way could be to group performance-related sub-questions by current products and services.

You typically need to choose between these groupings to avoid overlap of sub-questions, so ask yourself which will be the easiest cut to answer.

Check also that each sub-question is not in effect a rephrasing of another sub-question. Delete any direct repeats but do not remove sub-questions that are a legitimate sub-question of another sub-question, as per the example questions relating to travel from New York City to D.C. earlier in this chapter.

Be mindful of gaps either in topics or in the sub-question grouped under a certain topic. What is missing? What else would you need to know to bring insight to this topic? Test to see that the sub-questions you have would allow for all viable hypotheses and solutions related to the topic.

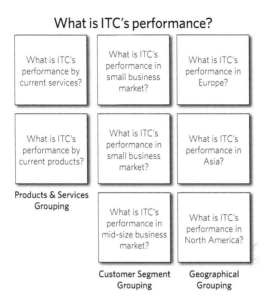

What is ITC's performance?

What is ITC's performance by current services?	What is ITC's performance in small business market?	What is ITC's performance in Europe?
What is ITC's performance by current products?	What is ITC's performance in small business market?	What is ITC's performance in Asia?
Products & Services Grouping	What is ITC's performance in mid-size business market?	What is ITC's performance in North America?
	Customer Segment Grouping	**Geographical Grouping**

Figure 8: Example grouping of sub-questions

Then step back and ask: taken together, would these sub-questions answer the overall question? That is, are the sub-questions collectively exhaustive, with no gaps?

STRUCTURING SUB-QUESTIONS: THE QUESTION TREE

Now that you have a set of sub-questions, grouped by topic, it's time to structure them into an integrated system: the D$_1$efine Question Tree.

Many consulting organizations use question trees to structure thinking and conduct analytical problem solving. This was certainly the case when I worked at McKinsey & Company. At the outset of each new project we used the process of creating a question tree as the way to open up the problem at hand and create structure for the work to be done.

Building a tree is about finding ways to group your sub-questions logically, by topic. As you move to the right on your tree, your sub-questions become more detailed. This means that within a topic area, you also want to organize your questions into different levels of detail, with those of the same level of detail sitting within the same vertical tier.

In each tier you typically want between two and eight questions. Without at least two sub-questions, you have not broken anything down. If you have more than eight sub-questions it gets hard to manage and you will usually find that the sub-questions are not all of same level and so fit more comfortably on different tiers.

Beware of inadvertently repeating a sub-question on the following tier. This can easily happen with different phasing and wording but which doesn't mean anything distinct, nor add anything new to the question it feeds into.

Within a tier, you order the sub-questions based on the order in which you would seek to answer them, acknowledging that some sub-questions will be answered in parallel and some require that you answer other sub-questions first before they can be addressed.

For every tier of your question tree, the sub-questions of that tier must not overlap, that is they are mutually exclusive, and when taken together, they must comprehensively address the question that feeds into the next tier, that is they have no gaps and are thus collectively exhaustive.

With no gaps and overlaps your tree is **mutually exclusive** and **collectively exhaustive**, a principle also referred to as **MECE**.

KEY CONCEPT: MECE

MECE, pronounced "me-see", is a grouping principle where information is arranged by separating a set of items into subsets that are mutually exclusive and collectively exhaustive.

- No gaps to ensure all factors are considered.

- No overlaps to ensure all key questions are separated.

A MECE approach helps encompass both the big picture and smaller details and this is one of the reasons why it is invaluable for strategic problem solving.

EXAMPLE QUESTION TREES

Let's return to Question 1: What is the most time- and cost-efficient way to get from New York City to Washington D.C. leaving tomorrow morning and arriving by 2pm?

We could translate Question 1 and 1.1 to 1.3 into a simple question tree (i.e. one tier):

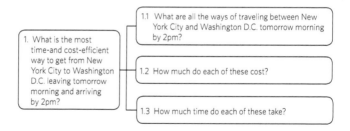

1.1 What are all the ways of traveling between New York City and Washington D.C. tomorrow morning by 2pm?

1. What is the most time-and cost-efficient way to get from New York City to Washington D.C. leaving tomorrow morning and arriving by 2pm?

1.2 How much do each of these cost?

1.3 How much time do each of these take?

Figure 9: Question 1, example tree

Or we could take Question 2 and similarly translate it into a question tree:

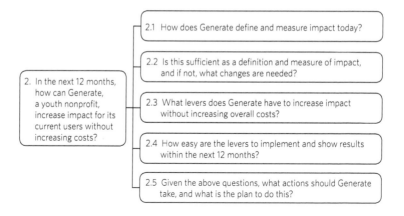

2.1 How does Generate define and measure impact today?

2.2 Is this sufficient as a definition and measure of impact, and if not, what changes are needed?

2. In the next 12 months, how can Generate, a youth nonprofit, increase impact for its current users without increasing costs?

2.3 What levers does Generate have to increase impact without increasing overall costs?

2.4 How easy are the levers to implement and show results within the next 12 months?

2.5 Given the above questions, what actions should Generate take, and what is the plan to do this?

Figure 10: Question 2, example tree

Now let's take a new example question, Question 3: How can Roberts sustainably increase profit by $100k per year by 2018?

A classic tree structure for a question about increasing profitability is organized around opportunities to increase revenue and opportunities to reduce costs.

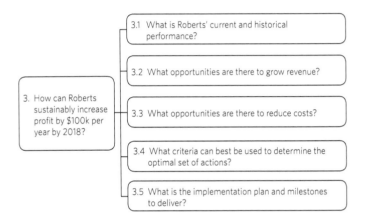

Figure 11: Question 3, example tree A

In the example above, the two sub-questions on revenue and costs (sub-questions 3.2 and 3.3) are couched between questions to understand the context and current situation (sub-question 3.1) and the implementation to deliver these (sub-questions 3.4 and 3.5).

The same Question 3 could also be translated into a tree organized into sub-questions around customer needs, market dynamics and competitors, as per the example tree overleaf:

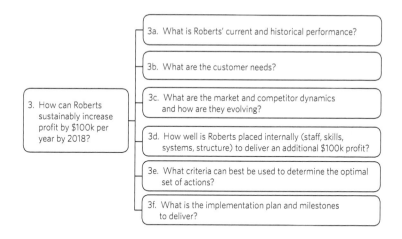

3. How can Roberts sustainably increase profit by $100k per year by 2018?

- 3a. What is Roberts' current and historical performance?
- 3b. What are the customer needs?
- 3c. What are the market and competitor dynamics and how are they evolving?
- 3d. How well is Roberts placed internally (staff, skills, systems, structure) to deliver an additional $100k profit?
- 3e. What criteria can best be used to determine the optimal set of actions?
- 3f. What is the implementation plan and milestones to deliver?

Figure 12: Question 3, example tree B

Remember, there is no right tree, but there are some wrong ones, where the tree is not MECE.

It is worth testing the number of tiers of sub-questions required for your tree. This tends to be no fewer than two tiers and is determined by whether the sub-questions are of a manageable scope or whether they need to be broken down into smaller components to better organize the work to be done.

For example, working with tree A from Figure 11, take sub-question 3.2: What opportunities are there to grow revenue? This is unlikely to be of manageable scope to answer directly. One way to break it down would be to add sub-questions exploring opportunities to increase price, or to increase volume.

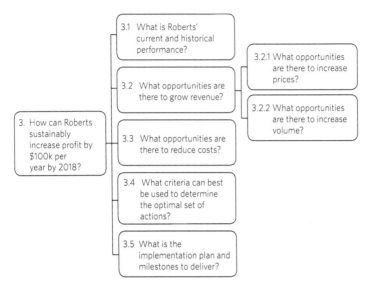

Figure 13: Question 3, example tree A with two tiers, v.1

Alternatively, question 3.2 could also be broken down into growing revenue both from existing customers and new customers:

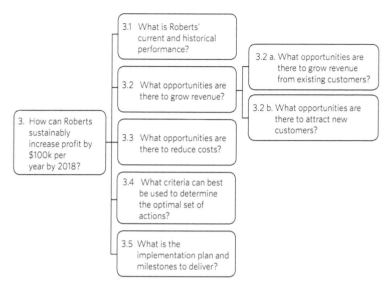

Figure 14: Question 3, example tree A with two tiers, v.2

Often, you may start to build your tree one way, then as it develops, you might reshuffle the groupings. In some cases, sub-questions that were in tier two or three may become tier one sub-questions, and vice versa. You may also add or rewrite questions to ensure the tree is completely MECE.

If you have written your sub-questions on Post-it® notes, you can gather together the strategy design team and move the questions around on a wall or whiteboard where everyone can see them and comment on the different structures.

Don't be afraid to take a break and come back to the tree with a fresh perspective. It matters to get it right since the tree maps out the domain of the possible solution and the work to be done. When the structure and organization of the tree works, teams often report that the sense of a "click" takes place. Once this happens, and the tree is complete, just as for your overall question—bar exceptional circumstances—it should not change.

STRATEGY IN 5D QUESTION TREE GROUPING

Earlier I mentioned there is never just one way to structure a D_1efine Question Tree. That said, I often find that for strategy questions a helpful way to structure the D_1efine Question Tree is one that aligns with the subsequent steps in Strategy in 5D i.e. steps D_2 to D_5. (It is unnecessary to cover step D_1 in the tree as the tree, along with the D_1efine Question Frame, completes what is required for step D_1).

In all trees, the sub-questions of tier one collectively need to address your overall question. If you structure your tree to align with Strategy in 5D, then the tier one sub-questions should collectively also give you all the key questions you need to complete each of the steps D_2 to D_5.

As in all other question trees, tier one cannot have more than eight sub-questions. Since you want at least one sub-question for each of steps D_2 to D_5, then you will have a minimum of four tier one sub-questions.

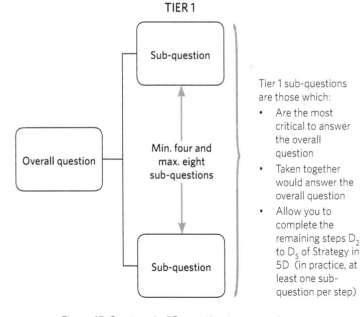

Figure 15: Strategy in 5D question tree grouping

65

Start by brainstorming all the questions you would like to ask in order to answer your overall question. Which step do they fit? Are they part of understanding where you are today (step **D₂iagnose**) or part of what you need to do to deliver (step **D₅eliver**)?

Organize your sub-questions by step and within each step, by level of detail, with the least detailed sub-questions in tier one. Then step back and check your tier one sub-questions to see if:

1. Collectively they answer the overall question.
2. In answering them all, you would complete steps **D₂** to **D₅** of Strategy in 5D.
3. They don't overlap and none are the repeat of a sub-question in a lower tier, or of the overall question.

Below is a recap of the key questions you need to address to complete each of the steps **D₂** through **D₅**:

- **D₁efine:** What is your goal and end point?
- **D₂iagnose:** What is your current situation and starting point?
- **D₃evelop:** What are all the viable options to reach your goal?
- **D₄ecide:** What is the best set of options to reach your goal?
- **D₅eliver:** What is your plan to deliver?

Following are some ideas for the types of questions that might be relevant for each step:

D₂iagnose sub-questions:

- They enable you to determine your starting point, and the customer, industry and competitor trends, which influence what your best strategic options will be.
- They relate to the internal situation within the organization and the external environment which the organization operates in.
  - The internal situation helps you understand the current mission, vision, strategy and values of the organization, its current and historical performance, and its skills, capabilities, technology and processes. Include any projections for the future, for example knowledge of forthcoming opportunities or of existing contracts up for renewal.

- The external situation covers the historical, current and future trends of the environment in which your organization operates. This includes regulation, economic growth, demographics, and political stability. Include anything known or projected for the future, e.g. a known or expected change in regulation, or trends in customer needs and the expected implications of these.
- Often tier one may include two sub-questions on step D_2iagnose, one on the internal situation and one on the external situation, with the more detailed topics and questions listed above in tier two and beyond.

D_3evelop sub-questions:

- Are answered once step D_2iagnose is complete and thus build on the diagnosis findings.
- Address areas to be explored when looking for viable options to answer your overall question.
- In a for-profit organization, these sub-questions often ask for ways to grow through new products/services, new customers and new geographies and look at options to reduce cost.

D_4ecide sub-questions:

- Express the criteria to be considered as you make your decisions such as impact, ease of implementation, risk, dependencies, which options fit well together and which don't.
- These may also include a sub-question on how to determine the criteria you'll use to select the set of options that will become your strategy.

D_5eliver sub-questions:

- Consider what it will take for the strategy to be implemented.
- This includes staff, skills, processes, technology, investments plus the delivery of milestones that will be necessary.

DOCUMENTING YOUR D$_1$EFINE QUESTION TREE

You can document your tree visually, just as you have it displayed on your whiteboard or wall. Alternatively, you can translate it into grouped lists of sub-questions.

Since it can get fiddly to visually document all the tiers of the tree on paper, I like to depict tier one of my tree visually as a tree and then write out tiers two onwards as a grouped list.

Following is an example tree for ITC displayed visually for the first tier in Figure 16 and then followed by the full tree with sub-questions grouped in prose:

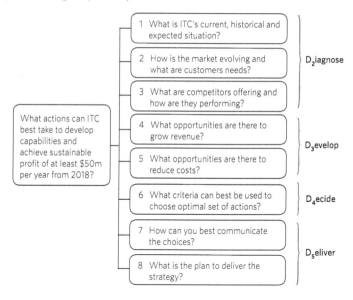

Figure 16: Example D$_1$efine Question Tree for ITC, first tier only

To make the prose easier to read, where a step has more than one tier one sub-question, then topic areas for each tier one sub-question have been added:

D$_2$iagnose:

Situation
1. What is ITC's current, historical and expected situation?
   1.1. What is ITC's stated mission, vision and strategy?
   1.2. What is ITC's current and historical financial performance?
   1.3. What is ITC's organizational structure and key operations?
   1.4. What are known facts about the future?
   1.5. What can ITC expect or see as possible in the future, if they assume continuing as they are today?

Customer needs
2. How is the market evolving and what are customer needs?
   2.1. What customer needs are ITC currently fulfilling?
   2.2. Are there other customer needs ITC know about or could foresee?
   2.3. What is the market size, trends and projected growth?
   2.4. Are there known or possible changes in regulation?

Competitors
3. What are competitors offering and how are they performing?
   3.1. Who are ITC's competitors?
   3.2. What is their current and historical performance, or what are their stated projections or growth plans?
   3.3. What products/services do they offer, what are the features/pricing, and what do we know about their future offerings?

Step D$_3$evelop:

Revenue

4. What opportunities are there to grow revenue?
   4.1. What opportunities are there to provide more of the current products and services to existing customers, and what could this deliver financially?
   4.2. Who and where are the most promising new customers to sell current products and services, and what could this deliver financially?
   4.3. What new products or services could ITC provide to meet the needs of existing customers, and what could this deliver financially?
   4.4. What new products or services could ITC provide to meet the needs of new customers, and what could this deliver financially?

Cost

5. What opportunities are there to reduce costs?
   5.1. What cost reduction opportunities are there in how ITC serve the customer?
   5.2. What cost opportunities are there when rethinking how ITC support customer-facing work?

Step D$_4$ecide:

Criteria

6. What criteria can best be used to choose optimal set of actions?
   6.1. What is the financial potential of each opportunity?
   6.2. What are the limitations, that is, what is the opportunity dependent on?
   6.3. How easy is each to implement?
   6.4. What is the level of risk of each and how can this be mitigated?
   6.5. What combinations are possible and how to they weigh up the above criteria assessed individually i.e. financial potential, limitations, ease of implementation and risk?

Step D₅eliver:

Communication

7. How can you best communicate the choices?
    7.1. Who needs to be communicated to?
    7.2. What is the purpose of the communication and the desired outcomes?
    7.3. What does each audience need?
    7.4. What medium should be used, how many meetings are required and where should these be?
    7.5. Who should present, with what material?
    7.6. What is the timing?

Implementation plan

8. What is the plan to deliver the strategy?
    8.1. What needs to change in terms of how we reach and serve customers?
    8.2. What needs to change in terms of our offering?
    8.3. What new skills are required, are these trainable or require new staff or both?
    8.4. What technology is required and by when?
    8.5. How does this translate into workstreams and align with existing plans?
    8.6. What is the role of the Delivery Office and/or other governance?
    8.7. How can plans best be adapted and piloted and then revised accordingly for another round of testing?
    8.8. How can progress best be tracked?

I use the creation of my D₁efine Question Tree to begin a document that I call the *Discovery Document*. For now I include the D₁efine Question Frame followed by the D₁efine Question Tree, but later in the process it becomes the repository for all the findings. Excerpts of the *Discovery Document* for ITC are contained in this and subsequent chapters. A full version can be downloaded at www.insightconsults.com.

THE TREE THAT BLOSSOMS

From the multitude of questions you first gathered, you now have a structure connecting all your sub-questions.

Your D_1efine Question Tree holds a map of all possible solutions to your overall question. It will provide you and your organization with a dynamic way of working through these issues strategically, creatively and logically.

As your work progresses, you will want to come back and review your tree, along with your D_1efine Question Frame—that is all the work you have done to complete Strategy in 5D step **D_1efine**—to ensure you do not miss any potential solutions.

D$_1$EFINE QUESTION TREE CHECKLIST

- Everything in your tree is expressed as a question and is as clear and concise as possible.

- There are no more than eight sub-questions in tier one (otherwise these need to be restructured into other tiers).

- No sub-question in any tier is a restatement of the overall question (or of any other sub-question).

- In every tier, all questions are distinct from one another, with no overlaps (mutually exclusive).

- The questions taken together cover all possible sub-questions (collectively exhaustive).

- If you were to answer all the questions in tier one, you would answer the overall question; similarly answering all the questions in tier two would answer all tier one questions, and so on...

- Key stakeholders have been involved in generating, or at least reviewing the D$_1$efine Question Tree.

- Key stakeholders are aligned behind your D$_1$efine Question Tree.

D_1efine

D_2iagnose

D_3evelop

D_4ecide

D_5eliver

2.1

DIAGNOSE YOUR SITUATION

*"Facts are stubborn things; and whatever may
be our wishes, our inclinations, or the dictates
of our passion, they cannot alter the state of
facts and evidence."*

John Adams

Strategy in 5D

Step	Chapter	Actions
D₁efine	1.1 Define Your Goal	Articulate goal as question ↓ Brainstorm sub-questions ↓
	1.2 Map Your Domain	Structure sub-questions
D₂iagnose	2.1 Diagnose Your Situation	Gather facts / Draw insights / Share findings
D₃evelop	3.1 Generate Hypotheses	Develop hypotheses ↓ Gather evidence ↩
	3.2 Test Hypotheses	Repeat until hypotheses confirmed or disproved ↓ Draw insights ↓ Share findings
D₄ecide	4.1 Make Choices	Review combinations ↓ Debate scenarios ↓
	4.2 Write Your Strategy	Document choices
D₅eliver	5.1 Communicate Your Strategy	Communicate strategy ↓ Pilot approach ↓
	5.2 Deliver Results	Adapt approach ↓ Track progress

ARC at every step

KEY IDEAS

With your D$_1$efine Question Frame and D$_1$efine Question Tree in place, you are ready to switch gears and start the second step **D$_2$iagnose**. By working through the sub-questions related to the **D$_2$iagnose** step (sub-questions 1 through 3 and their subordinates 1.1 through 3.3 in ITC's case), you will map the dynamics within and external to your organization. By working with your stakeholders to answer these sub-questions, you will be able to review your findings together and come to a shared diagnosis of the situation.

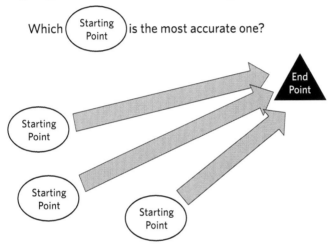

Figure 17: Need a clear starting point to determine right actions and path

An in-depth diagnosis requires you to dig below the surface and make connections between and draw inferences from diverse pieces of information. This in turn enables you to determine a clear starting point for the actions of your strategy which you will determine in the next step **D$_3$evelop** and later be prepared to make strong, informed choices in the fourth step, **D$_4$ecide**.

If you are developing a strategy for an organization you know well, you may be tempted to skip this step, thinking you know what the current situation is—but do you really want to gamble the future of your organization on what you think you know? If you misdiagnose your starting point then the actions you choose for your strategy will not be the right ones and will not deliver your goal.

It is likely that your stakeholders will offer their view of the current situation at the beginning of a strategy process. However, never assume that your combined views comprise a complete set of information. I have lost count of the number of times I have been told information about an organization's financial performance only to later discover that this information was incorrect when I looked at the facts in their financial statements.

A thorough and rigorous diagnosis requires assessing the full set of facts without bias or assumption. It also requires being open to new facts that may change your previous view of reality.

It is not uncommon to discover information that appears inconsistent and from this, you will need to determine what the most accurate view and diagnosis of the current situation is. This may be based on the reliability of different sources or on the weight of evidence leaning in one direction more than another.

EXAMPLE: DIAGNOSING THE SITUATION

Let's say your goal is to increase profit by $2m. You know quality is very important to customers. Without gathering more facts, you assume that any reduction in cost will not be tenable, due to concerns about them affecting quality and thus make revenue your sole focus.

Your set of actions will then be about ways to increase revenue. But what if you were to gather information and discover that costs had been reduced 10% over the past three years with no impact to quality and indeed that your top 10 customers had all reported improvements in quality.

Suppose also, customer feedback showed that beyond a certain quality threshold, customers got what they needed quality-wise and didn't need—or want—to pay for any more. Then it would be limiting to exclude reducing costs as a potential action relevant to your strategy.

You may want or need to supplement facts with interviews, such as with staff, market experts or customers, to add richness and test inconsistencies. When you communicate your findings, ensure that you are clear what is fact and what is interview-based feedback.

A rigorous diagnosis also requires you to think without cognitive biases[10]. This refers to work that has been done in Decision Science that demonstrates how susceptible we are to flawed and biased thinking. An example is confirmation bias, which leads us to see what we expect to, rather than what is actually there. This means that instead of objectively analyzing the information we gather, we instead assume it tells us what we expect.

By understanding some of the main cognitive biases that we fall prey to, we can learn to identify our own biases and objectively compensate for them. As a result, we become more effective decision makers.

You need to describe and document your diagnosis in a way that is easy to understand and that highlights what is most important, without information overload.

Your audiences need to understand the implications of what you are sharing and why it is important. Otherwise, they will make their own inferences and not necessarily those you intend. This makes it your job to make it clear why each piece of information is relevant and to connect the dots between seemingly disparate pieces of information.

Do not jump straight into finding and collating information. At the outset, be sure to create a workplan listing required information and sources with clear responsibilities and timings. In a 10 to 14 week-long strategy design process, the **D$_2$iagnose** step should take no longer than two weeks, so as to leave at least three times as long on the **D$_3$evelop** step.

DELIVERABLES, CONCEPTS, ARC AND MEETINGS

Step	Chapter	Key Concepts	Deliverables
D₂iagnose	2.1 Diagnose Your Situation	Dummy deck One message per slide Cognitive biases: ASCOSCA (Ask Oscar!) SWOT and PESTLE The Minto Pyramid Principle®	D₂iagnosis Information Table D₂iagnosis Document

Examples of applying ARC for diagnosing your situation are:

- Sources have been identified making the gathering of the information **actionable.**
- Information is researched and presented fairly and **rigorously.**
- Information is shared and implications are discussed **collaboratively.**

The key meetings required to complete this chapter are:

- Strategy design team: First meeting to identify information to be gathered through review of question tree. Second and third meetings to review information gathered.
- Steering committee: Review D₂iagnosis Document, identify any further work to be done to complete D₂iagnosis.

IDENTIFYING THE INFORMATION YOU NEED

To identify what information you need, return to your list of sub-questions. Reread all your tier one sub-questions that relate to the diagnosis. Then also read their sub-questions in tier two and any further tiers. For ITC, this would be sub-questions 1, 2 and 3 and their sub-questions 1.1 through 3.3 on page 69.

To generate the list of information needed, have the D₂iagnosis sub-questions from the tier furthest to the right in front of you (so for ITC these are the tier two sub-questions 1.1 through 3.3) and then work through each sub-question linearly to determine the information required to answer it. You can do this as a team, with the sub-questions on a whiteboard and the team in brainstorm mode. Or you can ask the team to prepare Post-it® notes detailing the information required to answer the sub-questions and be ready to share these with the team. Post-it notes work well here as you can put them on the wall for all to see, you can move them around to group by topic, and if they overlap, you can literally put them one atop the other.

You also want to identify sources for each piece of information, which you can either add simultaneously as you identify each piece of information or you can add once you have your full list of required information. Since most of the information you need is facts, finding sources should be straightforward, such as retrieving financial reports from the finance department. In a few cases, such as when you need information on competitors, or when looking at future trends, your sources may include discussions with, and information provided by colleagues, for example, talking to colleagues who formerly worked for a competitor. If there are any gaps in identifying the information required or their sources, be explicit about these and ask your stakeholders for input.

You can document the required information by sub-question in a **D$_2$iagnosis Information Table**. Overleaf is an example for ITC. In the left hand column are all the D$_2$iagnosis sub-questions from tier two (the tier furthest to the right for ITC). Each sub-question has its own row since specific information will be required to answer each. In the middle column, you have a list of required information and in the right hand column you have sources for this information.

D$_2$IAGNOSIS INFORMATION TABLE		
Sub-Questions	Required Information	Source
1.1 What is ITC's stated mission, vision and strategy?	• Mission statement • Values • Written strategy (if exists)	• CEO's office • Corporate Comms
1.2 What is ITC's current and historical financial performance?	• Profit & Loss (P&L) statement, balance sheet and cash flow for past three years, split by Business Unit (BU) • Projected budget and performance for this year and any future years • List of key customers by BU, revenue, profit and percentage of BU total	• Finance Team • BU Directors • Sales and Commercial Directors
1.3 What is ITC's organizational structure and key operations?	• Organizational diagram including key job titles and holders	• HR

D$_2$IAGNOSIS INFORMATION TABLE		
Sub-Questions	Required Information	Source
1.4 What are known facts about the future?	• Contracts up for tender with size (\$) and date • Known personnel changes • Known IT system changes • Known end of office leases	• Commercial Managers • HR • IT • Property Team
1.5 What can ITC expect in the future if they continue as they are today?	• Assumptions for future growth which develop based on known customers, insights from historical performance and customer insights • Extrapolate financial performance for next three years	• Strategy design team, based on review of information gathered in 1.1 to 1.4 and also in 2.1 and 2.2
2.1 What customer needs are ITC currently meeting?	• Preliminary list of customer needs	• Brainstorm and interviews with colleagues serving customers
2.2 Are there other customer needs ITC know about or could foresee?	• Feedback from customer surveys • Customer interviews, testing list of needs	• HR • Interview at least six customers

D$_2$IAGNOSIS INFORMATION TABLE		
Sub-Questions	Required Information	Source
2.3 What are market trends, current market size and projected growth?	• Definition of markets in which ITC plays today, plus their size today and projections, ideally for next three years	• Government data • Industry and analyst reports
2.4 Are there known or possible changes in regulation?	• List of any known or expected changes in regulation, complied from both team brainstorm and review online	• Team brainstorm • Review online
3.1 Who are ITC's competitors?	• List of competitors with: – size ($) – number of employees – key locations	• Competitor websites and annual reports • Press reports
3.2 What are the competitors' current and historical performance and any stated projections or growth plans?	• Profile per competitor listing: – Key customers – Revenue and profit for past three years – Any information on strategy and growth plans	• Interviews with colleagues who are former employees of competitors • Internet searches

D$_2$IAGNOSIS INFORMATION TABLE		
Sub-Questions	Required Information	Source
3.3 What products/ services do they offer, what are the features and pricing, and what do we know about their future offerings?	• Add to each competitor profile: - Core products and services offering - Key features and pricing • List any information about future plans	• Interviews with colleagues who are former employees of competitors

You can document the D$_2$iagnosis Information Table in Word or Excel. On my courses I find that some participants are more familiar with Word and prefer it although Excel makes it easier to sort the data, especially if you have a lot of information in your table. For presentation purposes, you can also copy a spreadsheet or parts of a spreadsheet into a Word document or a PowerPoint slide.

ORGANIZING THE WORK TO BE DONE

Now organize who will do what and by when. Typically, it works well for the team to work together on certain research tasks, although you always want one person with overall responsibility for each deliverable. Where possible let the strategy design team choose areas of particular interest to them. This does not have to be the areas they know best and in fact, given the propensity for cognitive biases (more about these later), it can actually work better to gather facts in an area where you have limited knowledge. So plan to discuss responsibility and timing as part of the strategy design team meeting where required information and sources are identified.

To document this you want to add owner and timing to your D_2iagnosis Table. If you are using Excel, I would encourage you to add two new columns as this will allow you to sort and filter the data by owner and timing. If you are not using Excel and have limited space, as is the case here, then you can add this information to the "Source" column, as per the below excerpt of a D_2iagnosis Information Table for ITC.

D₂IAGNOSIS INFORMATION TABLE (EXCERPT)		
Sub-questions	Required Information	Source
1.1 What is ITC's stated mission, vision and strategy?	• Mission statement • Values • Written strategy (if exists)	• CEO's office • Corporate Comms *James* *14th Jan*

The full version of the D_2iagnosis Information Table for ITC, including owner and timing for each piece of information can be found in the example *Discovery Document* for ITC at www.insightconsults.com.

DOCUMENTING YOUR FINDINGS IN A DUMMY DECK

Determine upfront how you will document your findings. You want to make this as simple as possible while ensuring your findings will be accessible and that all sources of information are clearly cited.

If you are familiar with using slides to communicate information then ask each owner to put their core findings into a handful of slides. Later we will discuss how to make the slides really compelling, but for now it suffices to get the relevant information onto slides.

You can mock-up what you anticipate to be on your slides together as a team. That way you can be clearer about what you expect to get back from each owner.

At McKinsey & Company, we called this a **dummy deck** or dummy pack. It comprises the title of each slide—which is your best informed guess of the likely finding—plus a note of the information you will be providing on each slide to support your title finding.

You can do this directly in PowerPoint although I find it easier to start with a piece of paper, dividing it into 9 or 12 rectangles. I use this as a mock-up for the flow and structure of my dummy slides. I like to handwrite this information to keep full focus on the overall structure and flow. If I write directly in PowerPoint, I lose this full focus, as I get distracted by details such as formatting. Since I inevitably change the order of my slides, their titles and what is written on them, I also write in pencil.

You want to have **one message per slide**—and not more. For example, suppose you know that you want to review revenue growth over the past three years. Then you will want a slide that displays revenue information and has space for a title so you can pull out the key finding. This ensures clarity of message. Since you don't know what the revenue growth will be, your best approach is to assign a title such as: *Revenue has grown by [Y%] over the past three years* and use square brackets plus a letter (here Y) to denote the unknown. You will fill in the unknown once you have information and can update and fill in your dummy slides.

You need to list on the body of the slide how you will present the information. In the slides overleaf, the information in square brackets on the body of each slide explains the format of the information to be presented, for example: text, line chart, bar chart, quotes. You also want to add the owner for the slide—as has been done shaded in gray on the right hand side of the subsequent dummy slides.

Once you have gathered and reviewed the information, you may want to change the title as well as fill in any square brackets in the title. You'll likely find that some titles are completely wrong—for example maybe revenue did not grow at all in the past three years.

It may also be that you want to highlight a more specific finding, for example: *Revenue has grown at a consistent [X%] for each of the past three years,* or *Total revenue growth has been [Z%] the past three years, masking swings between single and double digit growth.*

Once I have an overview of my slide titles and core content, and I've played around with the order and content until it flows, I then translate it into dummy slides in PowerPoint.

Provided you are willing to continue to change titles—and indeed scrap slides and/or add new ones—a dummy deck is a fantastic instrument to ensure a consistent structure and a focus on the desired end product. Here are example dummy slides for ITC:

ITC's mission is to be the leading reseller and IT services provider in North America and Europe

James

[Mission statement and values]

Source: Company strategy documents   1

It's stated strategy, designed [X] years ago, focuses on being a reseller and not on services

[Key points from last documented strategy]

Source: Company strategy documents

2

Revenue has grown by [Y%] over the past three years

[Line chart of revenue by year, with % growth by year & overall]

Source: Management accounts

3

This comprises [Z%] growth with medium-sized business and [A%] decline with large business

[Line chart of revenue growth by customer size, last three years]

Source: Management accounts

4

Profitablity has grown by [B%] over the three years, with highest profits from customer segment [C]

James

[Line chart of profitability overall and by customer size]

Source: Management accounts

5

Revenue and profitability are projected to each grow at [D%] and [E%] respectively per year for next two years

[Budget table or chart, showing projections]

Source: Management accounts

6

Today [F] customers comprise [G%] of our revenue

[List of customers, revenue and profitability]

Source: BU accounts list; Management accounts

7

Of these [H] have contracts up for renewal in next three years

Tyler

[Table of contracts up for renewal, with date and likelihood of winning]

Source: BU accounts list; Management accounts; interviews with sales staff

8

The business is organized in a matrix structure with sales units and product/services units

Jennifer

[Organizational diagram]

Source: HR

9

ITC's market share in the small business market - the biggest market - is only [I%]

[Table or chart of markets and their size today, plus any projections]

Source: Management accounts; 2016 Gartner report on US IT market   10

The key customer needs served today are [L, J, K]

[List of customer needs]

Source: Interviews with sales staff; customer survey 2015; customer interviews   11

There is evidence to suggest [M] and [N] and may become [customer needs/bigger customer needs]

Saffron

[Detail M and N and their expected impact]

Source: Interviews with sales staff, customer survey 2015; customer interviews

12

There [are/are not] key regulatory changes expected over the next three years

Jennifer

[List of comments/quotes from web searches or interviews]

Source: Department of Commerce; internet searches

13

ITC has [O] key competitors, [P] of whom are growing fast

[Table of competitors, key financials and offerings]

Source: Department of Commerce; company websites   14

Competitors [Q] and [R] have quite [similar/different] strategies

[Details of strategies for each competitor]

Source: Staff interviews; company websites   15

97

The owner of each slide now needs to gather the information they require and refine their slides titles and slide content accordingly. It can also be that they needs to add or delete slides based on the information found.

Assign one member of the strategy design team to collate the completed slides and ask each owner to forward their completed slides to that person.

Then, with your dummy deck in place, you are ready to gather and analyze the required information.

MITIGATING FOR COGNITIVE BIASES

As you embark on your first phase of information gathering, it is important for everyone in the strategy design team (and beyond) to be aware of cognitive biases. These are the assumptions and mistakes in reasoning that we make unconsciously and which affect our decisions. They come into play in many ways including influencing what information we choose to seek and once we have information, how we assess it.

Traditionally, economists believed in the human being as a rational thinker, with facts and information carefully weighed before decisions were taken. Decision Science debunks this notion and describes many of the shortcomings of human decision-making. For example, research by Dr. Daniel Kahneman and Dr. Amos Tversky[11] found that many human decisions rely on automatic or knee-jerk reactions that are based on rules of thumb that we develop or have hard-wired into our brains.

In the book *Moneyball: The Art of Winning an Unfair Game*,[12] Michael Lewis tells the story of Oakland Athletics baseball team and how manager Billy Beane adopted an analytical, evidence-based approach to assembling a competitive baseball team. Despite Oakland Athletics having less money than other baseball teams, they were able to recruit more successfully.

The central premise is that the collective wisdom of insiders working with Oakland Athletics and other baseball teams was subjective and often flawed. Their conventional wisdom valued qualities such as speed and contact. Yet rigorous statistical analysis demonstrated that on-base percentage and slugging percentage were better indicators of offensive success—and these qualities were cheaper to obtain. By adopting a recruitment strategy based on targeting on-base percentage and slugging percentage, Billy Beane was able to cost-effectively assemble a winning team.

It's not easy to adopt a "Moneyball" approach. Defaults are very powerful and you may not work in an organization with an objective, data-driven decision process, which is what enabled Oakland Athletics to identify undervalued indicators of success. Even if you do work in a data-driven culture, if the data is contrary to conventional wisdom, people may not accept it and will resist changing their thinking.

What you are looking to do is to inoculate yourself against cognitive biases. This enables you to gather and assess information without bias, which in turn provides the best foundation for effective decision-making.

The following introduction of seven key biases serves as an initial "inoculation shot", to allow you to be aware of and mitigate for each of them as you design your strategy.

AVAILABILITY BIAS

Availability bias is the tendency to estimate the probability of events by how easy it is to think of examples of similar events. This can be influenced by how recent your memories of a similar event are, either through direct experience or through the media, and how emotionally charged they are. The ease with which an event comes to mind becomes a proxy in our minds for how likely it is to occur.

Take the following example:

A man under 45 years of age in the US or the UK is most likely to die as a result of (please check one):

☐ Terrorist attack
☐ Homicide
☐ Suicide

What did you respond?

If you replied terrorist attack or homicide, you would be in the majority. We hear a lot in the media about terrorist attacks and homicides, but quite tragically, suicide is the more frequent cause of death[14] and is the most common cause of death among men under 45 in the UK.[13]

STATUS QUO BIAS

All else being equal we tend to choose the familiar status quo option. The status quo is our reference point and any change from this point is typically perceived as a loss.

This can be seen in the difference in the people signing up for organ donation in Europe. In Figure 18 at the top, you see those countries where a minority (4% to 28%) of the population participates in the organ donor program and at the bottom, the countries where the majority (86% to 100%) participates.[15]

Participation in Organ Donor Programs

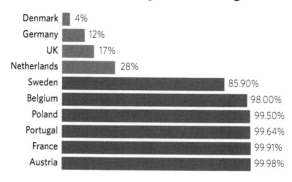

Figure 18: European country participation in organ donation

The four countries at the top have an opt-in for donor participation. That is, "Check the box if you want to participate in the organ donation program." Whereas the countries at the bottom have an opt-out, "Check the box if you don't want to participate in the organ donation program."

The Netherlands spends the most public money on campaigns to persuade people to participate, and got the highest participation rate among opt-in countries, but even that did not get them anywhere near the rates of opt-out countries. This is the power of the status quo bias at work.

Another fascinating example here is the UK vote to leave the EU in 2016. At first sight, status quo seems to be to "Remain" and many pundits expected Remain to win, in part due to status quo bias. Yet depending on your age, status quo is not necessarily with Britain part of the EU. Prior to 1973 Britain was not a member (of the then EEC) and this may reflect one reason why older voters were much more likely to vote "Leave" versus younger voters.

In strategy design work, a stakeholder often suggests a key action is to win big pieces of work or new clients in an existing market. Since this fits with the existing status quo, this is easy and uncontentious to suggest. Yet, it has not happened to date. So ask why? As Henry Ford said: "If you do what you have always done, you will get what you have always gotten". Applying this here, don't fall for a strategy that is what are you already doing unless what you are already doing delivers exactly you what you need.

CONFIRMATION BIAS

Simply put, it's easy to miss something you are not looking for. Even more so if implicitly you are expecting or wanting a certain result and so are predisposed to look for this in your information.

This is the essence of confirmation bias: the tendency to look for, interpret and remember information in a way that confirms our preconceptions.

This, for example, comes into play when describing an organization's financial performance. You may have a preconception of how the organization has performed and then cite information to support this, yet this information may only give a partial and potentially misleading picture of financial performance.

Daniel Kahneman coined the acronym WYSIATI, which is an abbreviation for "What you see is all there is". It captures the human tendency to passively accept the formulation given and to form impressions and judgments based on the information that is available to us.

WYSIATI can also play out by assessing information too quickly and superficially. In his book *"Thinking Fast and Slow"*[16], Dr. Kahneman uses the following example which I invite you to answer:

"A bat and a ball together cost $1.10. The bat cost $1.00 more than the ball. How much does the ball cost?"

_____

_____

_____

_____

Take a look in the Appendix, on page 315, and see how you fared. If you got it wrong, you are in good company: 50% of Havard and Yale students and 80% of students from other universities got it wrong too. This is WYSIATI thinking. It is fast, easy, comfortable and lets you come up with a quick answer or decision, but one that is often wrong.

Confirmation bias and WYSIATI can interfere when you are interviewing someone for information for your strategy. It shows in the questions you do and don't ask, and how consistently you ask follow-up questions to probe more deeply, versus accepting things at face value.

Hence the importance of asking what is missing from the information you have gathered and then filling in those gaps, and challenging yourself with the questions:

- What am I not asking?
- What am I not seeing?
- What information am I missing?

OVERCONFIDENCE BIAS

Read through the following table and provide estimates for each of the eight items, plus a lower and upper estimate where you are 90% confident that the actual number lies within this range:[17]

To estimate, all for 2015	Main Estimate	Low	High
1. GDP per capita in the US			
2. Proportion of books sold in electronic format in the US			
3. Proportion of American public school students qualifying for free or reduced school lunches			
4. Population of European Union			
5. Number of nations in the United Nations			
6. Your organization's worldwide revenue 2015			
7. Your organization's worldwide net assets, 31 December 2015			
8. Your organization's worldwide employee turnover 2015 (%)			

For how many of the eight questions do you think you provided a range within which the actual number falls?

Now go to the Appendix, on page 316, and take a look.

If you are like most people, then you will have been overconfident. Alpert and Raiffa's work showed that 42.6% of quantities fell outside of participants' 90% confidence ranges.[19]

You might expect this result to improve if you are a subject-matter expert. But it does not. The same or an even worse level of overconfidence pervades, as experts can be more convinced that they are right.[18]

In terms of your strategy design work, this means that whatever you do, seek full information and allow yourself to be surprised about what it is telling you.

SUNK COST BIAS

When we come to making a decision, we often consider effort and work already done as a criteria for making a decision. For example, suppose ITC has already done a lot of work to determine how to improve the quality of its customer service. This includes a plan to make the improvements and strong buy-in from staff to make this change. When ITC comes to decide which actions should be taken to meet the profit goals, should the work done on customer service be a factor in their decision? No. The question remains whether a higher quality customer service would create more profit. If you are emotionally invested in this option, can you see how easy it would be to argue for it? For example, "We can't stop now, otherwise what we've done will be lost." So pause, and ask yourself, what decision you would make if you had not invested anything yet. Would you really watch the second half of the movie if you had not already watched the first half?

CONTROLLABILITY BIAS

If we are in control of something we tend to associate less risk with it—for example we see less risk when we are driving than when someone else is. Or we see more risk in flying versus driving where we are not the one piloting the aircraft but would be driving the car.

This can translate to business too. For example, if a key customer's contract is up for renewal, research suggests that you will be more confident about retaining it if you are in charge of the renewal, rather than if one of your colleagues is in charge. Yet there is no rational evidence to back this up, so beware not to implicitly make this assumption as part of your findings.

ANCHORING BIAS

None of us start looking for information in a vacuum. We all have preconceptions, including those based on views shared by others.

Decision Science shows that we tend to rely too heavily on the first piece of information we hear. In practice this means that if, for example, we hear that competitors are focused on developing a certain technology, then we tend to look for information related to this fact, rather than looking more broadly.

In a price negotiation, the first person to name a price usually sets the range in which the final price will fall, as subsequent bids tend to oscillate around this first price. This means that being first to name a price for your next car, or for a company acquisition, is usually advantageous.

In their book *Blindspot: Hidden Biases of Good People*, Harvard Professor Mahzarin Banaji and University of Washington Professor Anthony Greenwald describe an experiment by Dan Ariely. He asked MIT students to write down the last two digits of their Social Security number and then to estimate the price of a trackball, an item familiar to them.

Amazingly, there was a substantial correlation between the two sets of numbers when logically there should have been none. For example, those with the last two digits of their Social Security number between 0 and 19 said they would pay an average of $8.62 for the trackball. This price increased upwards until those with a Social Security number ending between 80 and 99 offered $26.18 for the very same item.

So if you want to take a break for lunch at 1pm, be the first one to suggest a specific time, namely 1pm, for lunch. Due to anchoring bias, the ensuing discussion is most likely to focus on whether 1pm or another time would be best for lunch, rather than suggesting something totally different, like whether to have a lunch break at all.

CHECKING YOU HAVE MITIGATED FOR BIASES

As you gather your information and fill in your dummy slides, step back and review the list of cognitive biases above. Do any need to be mitigated? I use the acronym ASCOSCA (which I pronounce as "Ask Oscar!") to remind me of the biases to check for:

A vailability bias

S tatus quo bias

C onfirmation bias

O verconfidence bias

S unk cost bias

C ontrollability bias

A nchoring bias

What measures have you taken or will you take to mitigate the potential impact of the biases?

To rigorously inoculate yourself against these biases, a culture of constant awareness is required. To reinforce this, you can explicitly explain to the steering committee the measures you undertake to keep yourself from falling into these flawed ways of thinking. This will raise both your own awareness and gives stakeholders permission to remind you of your intention should your awareness slip. Similarly, make it part of the modus operandi of the strategy design team to question how information is collated and what efforts are made to inoculate against biases.

SWOT ANALYSIS

With the important information about cognitive biases in mind, let's look at two useful analytical tools. The first is a SWOT analysis (Strengths, Weaknesses, Opportunities, Threats)[20] which can be used as part of your diagnosis of the current situation. The idea is to assess information about your organization along the following four dimensions:

Strengths Internal characteristics of the organization which enable it to excel.

Weaknesses Internal characteristics of the organization which place it at a disadvantage.

Opportunities Aspects in the external environment which the organization could pursue to its advantage.

Threats Aspects in the external environment which could cause the organization problems.

A SWOT analysis is often a helpful way to communicate insights from and answers to your sub-questions and can be used to engage discussion and to align viewpoints.

It is often depicted in the form of a four-box matrix. Every point you add to the matrix needs supporting information that you can produce if asked.

SWOT	
Strengths	**Weaknesses**
Long-standing and trusted relationships with over 1000 customers Deep relationships with suppliers Strong employee loyalty and retention Effective sales model for serving large businesses	Over-reliance on large and medium business, with limited footprint in small business Little innovation over past five years while competitors have introduced new offerings Expensive sales models that are uneconomical for serving small business
Opportunities	**Threats**
Introduce low cost, modularized offering for medium and small business Expand business in Northern Europe, with focus on large business Extend existing end-of-life recycling offer Standardize process across BUs to reduce costs by 10%	Continued pressure on pricing and margins with large business Revenue stagnates or even falls relative to competitors Lose niche with large business and have no replacement Struggle to create a more cost effective model to serve small business

Figure 19: Example SWOT Analysis for ITC

PESTLE ANALYSIS

The second analytical tool is PESTLE (Political, Economic, Social, Technological, Legal, Environmental).[21] It can be very useful if your work on sub-questions includes looking in depth at the macroeconomic environment in which your organization operates:

Political The outlook and expected impact of central and local government and of tax, trade, labor and immigration policies.

Economic The outlook and expected impact of the economy including expected growth, inflation, interest rates and exchange rates.

Social Trends including demographics, consumer attitudes and lifestyles and their expected impact.

Technological The expected changes in technology including innovation and research funding, and their impact.

Legal The expected changes in legislation as well as impact of existing legislation including employment, patent and healthy and safety law.

Environmental[22] The outlook for the environment and the impact of this.

Conducting a PESTLE analysis often makes sense if you want to compare opportunities in different geographies. This is especially true if the geographies you are considering are less known to your organization or if they have potentially fast-changing political and economic situations.

You can lay out your PESTLE as a table with six boxes, analogous to the format for the SWOT analysis. I personally like a version that explicitly splits out commentary on each area and the expected impact and implications of it, as per the example for ITC in the UK, written prior to the EU referendum, which is overleaf:

PESTLE		
Area	Expected Trends	Expected implications
Political	• Stable UK government with pro-business agenda • EU exit is possible with unknown implications for trade[23]	• Nothing significant is expected besides possible EU exit • If exit the EU, consider whether UK remains an optimal location or whether another EU country becomes more favorable
Economic	• Generally solid economy, subject to global trends (as per all countries) • Expect continued low inflation and interest rates • Dollar expected to maintain strength against the pound	• Good economy means growing businesses which increases their IT needs, great for ITC • No other significant implications as not expecting big changes from present

PESTLE		
Area	Expected Trends	Expected implications
Social	• Population growth on average 0.7% 2004-2014, fastest in EU • Aging population	• Since ITC's customers are businesses, consumer trends tend to have less impact
Technological	• Fast innovation with digital economy, big data and Internet of Things (IoT) • Technology done well is a key differentiator for businesses	• Ride on this trend to highlight the need for technology • Will improve services and should reduce costs
Legal	• Legislation is part governed by EU, unless exit the EU, in which case all will become UK law over time	• Nothing significant expected in short-term
Environmental	• UK likely to experience more extreme weather, e.g. flooding, in the future	• Need to ensure services account for risk of more extreme weather

Figure 20: Example PESTLE analysis for ITC

COMPLETING YOUR DUMMY DECK

Once you have done your research—having mitigated for biases along the way—you can update your dummy deck, as you move towards creating your D$_2$iagnosis Document, and completing the **D$_2$** step.

A good set of slides rests on three things:

Structure of your presentation, as conveyed through the order and titles of your slides.

Content, as conveyed by the information on the body of each slide.

Design as conveyed in the layout and formatting of each slide.

To create a good set of diagnosis slides you need to do more than simply "fill in" your dummy slides. Reflect on your findings and how they necessitate updates to both the structure and content of your dummy slides. Put effort into a clean design so there is no distraction from the content you are sharing.

Start by looking at the structure of your dummy slides. Are all the key findings presented in the form of a slide title, or do new ones need to be added or superfluous ones removed? Do your slides flow or is there a more logical order? Which slide titles can be rewritten in a way that more precisely reflects your findings? Play around with both the order and the titles until all your key findings are reflected.

Now look at the content, that is the information on the body of each slide to support each slide title. Don't be limited by what you thought the evidence would be when you drew up your dummy deck; if you have found more compelling information, use it.

You also don't want to cram information onto a slide. Often less is more: choose the most impactful information and drop the rest. If the information really is relevant, then better to split it onto two slides, each with its own key message conveyed in its title.

Keep asking yourself if every piece of information is needed to support the title. If not, discard it or place it in an appendix. Never include information just to demonstrate that you've done the work.

When you present your slides, you want to add life with a voiceover replete with details and anecdotes. Do not however rely on your voiceover for communicating key messages, otherwise when your slides are emailed or shared—which happens more often that most of us anticipate—your key messages will be lost. So check that your slides work standalone: a colleague needs to be able to pick up your slides, read them and understand all your key findings.

The final key component for effective slides is design and formatting. Everyone is affected by how something looks. If a slide has a clean, simple design it's easier to take in. A poorly designed slide means your audience's energy is spent on deciphering the slide rather than focusing on what really matters—your content.

Do not underestimate the power of layout, colors and fonts to aid understanding. If you use the same layout, formatting and colors for all your presentations, your audience will be conditioned to know what to expect and can better navigate the slides regardless of the subject matter.

Consistency and accuracy convey a sense of professionalism which ensures no distraction from your messages. I remember a presentation early in my career, where I had a mistake in the numbers on one of the slides. I had a lackadaisical attitude towards formatting, believing that it was my ideas that mattered. But due to the mistake, the discussion got stuck on the erroneous number and never got back to the content and ideas I had been burning the midnight oil on. The error was a typo rather than an error in calculation, but it put a question mark over the accuracy of all my numbers and by extension on my overall findings. With the credibility of my work in question, key ideas were obscured by the client's understandable need to check all the numbers and figure out themselves what they meant. All the hard work I had put into it, only to be scuppered by a typo. Never again, I promised myself. Accuracy and formatting matters because it helps me get what I want: the audience solely focused on my content and thinking.

KEY CONCEPT: EFFECTIVE SLIDE DECKS

Structure

- Each slide has one message, which is the slide title.
- The order of your slides conveys your messages in a logical sequence.
- Taken together the slide titles contain all key findings.

Content

- Slide titles do not contain superfluous information, either better in the body of the slide or removed entirely.
- No slide title is longer than two lines.
- The information on the body of each slide provides sufficient evidence for its title.
- Every piece of information on the slide is either necessary to support the title or adds richness without distracting from the key message.
- No slide is over-crammed with information.
- Each slide works standalone, with no voiceover.

Design

Data is presented in a like-for-like way:
- The same time period is used when displaying financial information. For example, if you show a revenue line chart for the past three years, followed by one for profitability for the past five years, the mind will quickly compare the two lines assuming they represent the same time period.
- Where lack of data genuinely prevents use of a like-for-like time period then explicitly point this out to your audience so they don't inadvertently make an apples-with-apples comparison when it's an apples-with-oranges (or worse crocodiles) comparison.

Layout and frameworks are used consistently:

- Once you have introduced a way to lay something out, or have used a framework, then stick with it.

- If you present a table of information with each column representing a year, your audience's minds will automatically assume this to be the case with future tables. So don't then include a table with each year represented by a row

- Or suppose early in your slides you articulate three criteria you will use to make decisions, then later describe five totally different factors that led to a decision. This will be confusing. Use one or the other and stick to it.

Colors, shapes and fonts are used consistently:

- If you have used one color to represent one thing, e.g. blue for revenue, continue to do so. Don't then later use blue for profit. This will confuse the mind and possibly invoke a misreading of information.

- Similarly with shapes and symbols, if you use a rectangular shape to mean one thing, don't then introduce another thing using the same shape. This includes when you write text inside certain shapes.

- Use a consistent font and font size for titles, slide text and footnotes. Also ensure consistency in margin widths and box sizes throughout.

Slides are sleek, clean and accurate:

- Avoid lots of different images, colors and fonts. Only use complicated graphics if they genuinely highlight a point.

- Redesign any slides that don't look right. Small changes can make a big difference to clean design.

- Double-check for typos and where possible ask someone else to do a typo check for you.

COMPLETED DUMMY DECK FOR ITC

An example of a D_2iagnosis slide deck for ITC follows. This builds on the dummy deck you saw earlier in the chapter.

Several of the slides will seem familiar as they did not change dramatically from the dummy deck. In other parts of the deck, there are changes including:

- Additional slide: the dummy deck did not include a slide referring to the geographical source of revenue and profits; this is added as slide six.
- Different order: for better flow, the slide with the organizational diagram is moved to become the third slide before moving on to finance and customers.
- Revised title for slide four: the revised title now refers to current revenue as well as revenue growth, which ensures the audience is anchored to the correct starting number. The time period of the chart was extended to five years to both match the date of the strategy and to give a longer historical precedent.
- Revised title for slide seven (formerly slide six): it turned out that profit numbers were actually flat over three years rather than having risen.

For a D_2iagnosis slide deck for ITC, you could also add a SWOT analysis slide or PESTLE analysis slide.

ITC's mission is to be the leading reseller and IT services provider in North America and Europe

Mission Statement

To be North America and Europe's partner of choice for provision of IT products and services

Values

- Put the customer first
- Be the expert partner to our customers, using technology to help their businesses to grow
- Have a collaborative and meritocratic work environment

Source: Company strategy documents   1

It's stated strategy, designed five years ago, focuses on being a reseller and not on services

Strategy (2011)

- Grow share of large business segment products in North Americas
- Expand product business geographically across Europe from existing Western European base
- Develop and grow offerings for medium-sized businesses in North America

Source: Company strategy documents   2

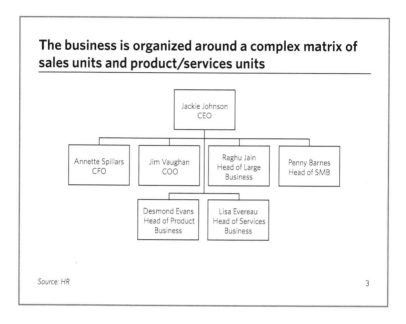

The business is organized around a complex matrix of sales units and product/services units

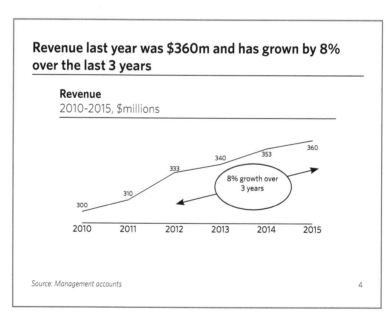

Revenue last year was $360m and has grown by 8% over the last 3 years

Revenue
2010-2015, $millions

This comprises 23% growth with medium-sized business and 4% decline with large business

Revenue split by Large, Medium and Small Businesses
$ millions

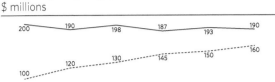

| 2010 | 2011 | 2012 | 2013 | 2014 | 2015 |

——— Large (>$500m revenue) ------ Medium ($7.5m to $500m)
·········· Small (<$7.5m revenue)

Source: Management accounts

5

80% Revenue and 85% Profit is from US

Revenue by Country
100% = $360 million

2015 Profit by Country
100% = $35 million

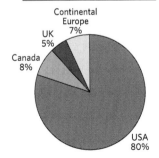

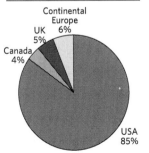

Source: Management accounts

6

Profitability flat last three years, comprising fall in large business profits and rise in small business

Profitability overall and split by customer segment
$ millions

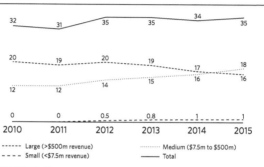

	2010	2011	2012	2013	2014	2015

- - - - - Large (>$500m revenue)   ·········· Medium ($7.5m to $500m)
- - - - Small (<$7.5m revenue)   —— Total

Source: Management accounts

7

Projected profitability growth 1%, 10% and 10% by segment resp. per year, yielding $42m profit

Profitability by segment
2016-2018 $m

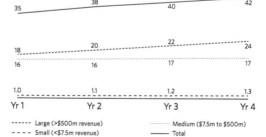

	Yr 1	Yr 2	Yr 3	Yr 4

- - - - - Large (>$500m revenue)   ·········· Medium ($7.5m to $500m)
- - - - Small (<$7.5m revenue)   —— Total

Source: Management accounts

8

Today 17 (11%) customers comprise 73% of our revenue

Customers and Profitability
2016, $ millions

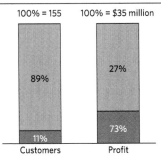

100% = 155   100% = $35 million

Customers: 89% / 11%
Profit: 27% / 73%

Customers   Profit

Source: BU accounts list; Management accounts

9

Of these 17 customers, 11 have contracts up for renewal in next 3 years

Customer	Name	2015 Revenue	2015 Profit	Contract Size	Start date	End date	Total length	Due up next 3 years
1	Spectrum	45.6	4.1	250	Oct-11	Sep-16	5 years	Y
2	Handy Andys	41.4	2.9	180	Jun-15	May-17	2 years	Y
3	Bellview Hotels	19.1	2.1	120	Nov-16	Oct-16	3 years	Y
4	Johnsons and Co	14.6	1.9	200	Jan-15	Dec-20	6 years	N
5	Advantage	16.7	1.5	60	Feb-15	Jan-18	3 years	Y
6	Decorum	17.3	1.3	85	Dec-14	Nov-18	4 years	Y
7	Furniture World	16.4	1.2	100	Mar-15	Feb-19	4 years	N
8	Ashton Breweries	12.8	1.2	25	Jul-14	Jun-16	2 years	Y
9	Kirkton and Jameson	12.0	1.2	95	Apr-13	Mar-18	5 years	Y
10	Alexander Enterprises	12.2	1.1	65	Apr-14	Mar-19	5 years	N
11	Infinitum	12.9	1.1	60	Sep-12	Aug-16	4 years	Y
12	Generation X	10.5	1.1	70	Nov-14	Oct-19	5 years	N
13	Experience Holidays	12.2	1.1	50	Dec-14	Nov-18	4 years	N
14	Spotlight	12.5	1.1	50	Oct-13	Sep-17	4 years	Y
15	Excalibur	13.4	1.1	40	Feb-15	Jan-18	3 years	Y
16	Wainwright	12.3	1.0	50	Oct-15	Sep-19	4 years	N
17	Younier Games	12.8	1.0	60	Jan-11	Dec-16	6 years	Y
		294.8	26.0	1560				
	Contracts up next 3 years	217	19	1025				
	%	73%	72%	66%				

Source: BU accounts list; Management accounts; interviews with sales staff

10

ITC's market share in the small business market - the biggest market - is less than 1%

Market Share, Large business
100% = $1.5 billions

13%

87%

Market Share, Medium business
100% = $2 billions

8%

92%

Market Share, Small business
100% = $1 billion

1%

99%

No market share in US above 15%

Source: Management accounts; 2016 Gartner report on US IT market

11

Customer needs served today include technical expertise and speed of supplying products

Customer needs served today

- Provision of up-to-date information and technical expertise on latest technology

- Seamless supply of products, and where required at significant speed

- Provision of IT services in cost-effective, reliable and seamless way

Source: Interviews with sales staff, customer survey 2015; customer interviews

12

New needs include provision of modularized services and cost-savings share billing model

Unserved or new customer needs

- Provision of modularized services with the ability to buy these à la carte
- Creation of cost-saving share model where savings enabled through IT services are shared
- Rental of IT products
- Recycling of end-of-life products

Source: Interviews with sales staff, customer survey 2015; customer interviews

13

No major regulatory changes expected although recycling regulations will increase needs

Expected regulation

- No expected legal changes affecting supply of products
- EU recycling regulation requires end-of-life equipment to be recycled and this creates a need which ITC could serve

Source: Department of Commerce; Internet searches

14

ITC has 3 major competitors, 2 of whom are growing fast

	ITC	Avantguard	Technology Partners	Minacon
Product and Services offering	Primarily product Large & medium businesses	Primarily service Mainly large businesses	Products with some services SMB focus	Product & services Large & medium businesses
Key customers	Spectrum Handy Andys	Bucaneer Tyrus	Agate Inc Vox Industries	Cyron Bank Tagent Group
Revenue 2015	$360m	$550m	$320m	$425m
Profit 2015	$35m	$70m	$30m	$42m
Profit margin (%)	9.7%	12.7%	9.3%	9.9%
Revenue growth last three years	8%	25%	11%	2%
Profit growth last three years	0%	32%	7%	3%
# Employees	1250	2200	980	1400
Key locations	San Francisco, New York, Miami	Minneapolis, Boston, Los Angeles	Chicago, Austin, Los Angeles	Seattle, Boston, Austin

Source: Department of Commerce; Internet searches

15

Avantguard and Technology Partners' growth shows success targeting different customer segments

- Avantguard has continued to grow in revenue with large businesses largely due to focus on growing services market (versus stagnant product market)

- Technology Partners has made it easy for small businesses to trade with them by having a very easy to use and informative web shop and a 24-hour customer services line.

- Both have picked a clear offering and target customers and then focused relentlessly on this

Source: Staff interviews; Company websites

16

STRUCTURING WITH MINTO PYRAMID PRINCIPLE®

With your dummy deck completed and your key findings documented, you want to draw out the implications of your findings, to move towards having a D_2iagnosis of your situation.

The Minto Pyramid Principle®, designed by Barbara Minto and described in her book *The Pyramid Principle*[24], provides an excellent way to structure your thinking. It can be used to organize your findings and help reveal their implications.

Let's start with a simple example: how would you remember the following list of items to pack for your vacation?

Did you group the items into categories, as below?

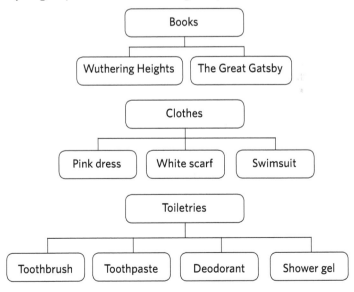

Figure 21: Example pyramid for things to pack

It is much easier to remember the three categories and the associated items than to remember the full list without any categorization. This is the approach of the Minto Pyramid Principle®, with information organized into groups and structured as pyramids to show the relationships between each item in the group.

In this example, the name of the group sits at the top of the pyramid and the associated items sit underneath. This reflects a key rule of the Minto Pyramid Principle®: each row of the pyramid comprises items of the same level or nature.

While our purpose in this chapter is to use The Minto Pyramid Principle® to reveal and structure our findings and implications, The Minto Pyramid Principle® can be used to structure almost any thinking or communication. The pyramid structure makes us think about and then makes explicits the links between different pieces of information. In the next section we use it to help reveal and then structure the implications of our D_2iagnosis findings.

GENERATING IMPLICATIONS

Start by listing each finding i.e. each slide title, on an individual Post-it® note and display them on a large whiteboard or wall. Where possible, arrange your Post-it® notes in a horizontal row. This represents that as findings, they are all of the same level or row.

Figure 22: Excerpt of Post-it® notes for ITC, showing findings

Then step back and ask yourself: what are the implications of your findings? What do the findings infer when considered in groups and considered collectively? For example, looking at findings on ITC's financial performance, what do they imply about likely future performance? Can you infer that the $50m profit goal for 2018 is likely to be met or missed?

Drawing out implications is an iterative process. You will come up with an initial set of implications when you first review your findings. Then as you discuss and think about what all the findings and implications mean, you will revise these and draw out additional or more precise implications.

Write your implications above the findings, drawing lines from the findings to the related implication(s), as per the following example for ITC:

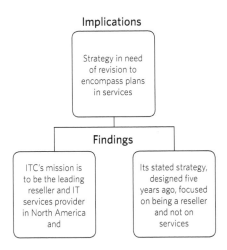

Figure 23: Example pyramid for ITC showing findings and implications

A second example pyramid on findings and implications of ITC's financials is below:

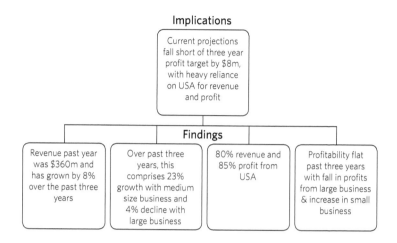

Implications

Current projections fall short of three year profit target by $8m, with heavy reliance on USA for revenue and profit

Findings

| Revenue past year was $360m and has grown by 8% over the past three years | Over past three years, this comprises 23% growth with medium size business and 4% decline with large business | 80% revenue and 85% profit from USA | Profitability flat past three years with fall in profits from large business & increase in small business |

Figure 24: Example pyramid for ITC showing findings and implications

There is no rule about how many implications will come from your findings. Multiple findings can lead to one implication, as shown in Figure 23 and Figure 24. A sole finding can also lead to multiple implications.

It is important not to over infer by trying to imply more than you have information to substantiate. For example, if 80% of your revenue comes from the USA, you can infer that ITC is heavily dependent on the USA today. But you can't infer that this dependence on the USA will be there in the future unless you know that there are no plans to grow revenue outside the USA.

Make sure that every implication really is an implication and not a restatement of a finding. This is analogous to your D$_1$efine Question Tree, where you don't want any question to be a restatement of another. Here no box in your pyramid can be a restatement of any other. For implications on financials, it is insufficient to say that revenue has grown 8% and that profit has been flat because this is a summary rather than the implication of the findings.

Be precise with your words so that each word conveys exactly what you mean, without ambiguity. If your thinking is not yet clear, do not try and fudge an implication with clever-sounding words which don't say much.

Ensure that statements of a similar nature are on the same row of the pyramid. In the example here we have findings in one row and implications in another, with each row supporting the information in the row above it.

You can put all your implications and findings together into one pyramid, where the overall implication would be at the top, the more detailed implications on the next row and the findings on the bottom row.[25]

Initially your overall implications box can be empty, as shown in Figure 25. To complete this box, repeat the same approach you used to generate implications from your findings and now applied to generate an overall implication from your implications. Step back and consider all the implications you have already identified and from there, tease out the overall implication.

Turn the page and look at the six implications in Figure 25 overleaf, which comprises Figure 23 and Figure 24 plus implications from the remaining diagnostic findings for ITC.

List below thoughts on what the overall implication of these could be:

_____

_____

_____

_____

_____

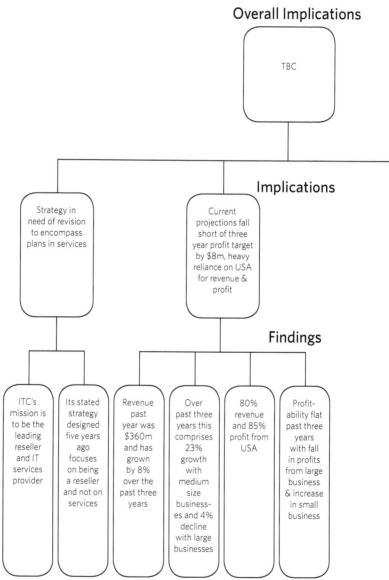

Figure 25: Example pyramid for ITC linking implications and findings

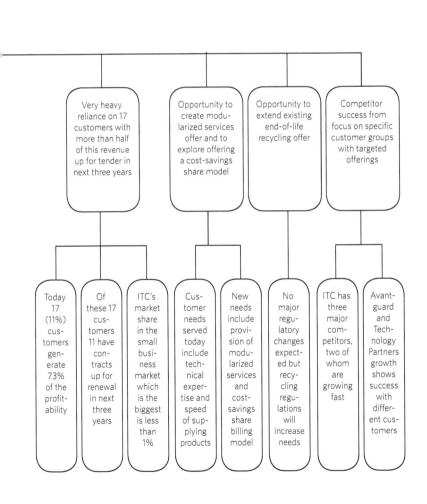

Very heavy reliance on 17 customers with more than half of this revenue up for tender in next three years			Opportunity to create modularized services offer and to explore offering a cost-savings share model	Opportunity to extend existing end-of-life recycling offer		Competitor success from focus on specific customer groups with targeted offerings	

| Today 17 (11%) customers generate 73% of the profitability | Of these 17 customers 11 have contracts up for renewal in next three years | ITC's market share in the small business market which is the biggest is less than 1% | Customer needs served today include technical expertise and speed of supplying products | New needs include provision of modularized services and cost-savings share billing model | No major regulatory changes expected but recycling regulations will increase needs | ITC has three major competitors, two of whom are growing fast | Avant-guard and Technology Partners growth shows success with different customers |

The overall implication I draw out for ITC from the six implications is:

> To meet $50m profit goal and close the $8m shortfall projected by our Corporate plan, ITC will need to both successfully win contract renewals and extend their range of services, and extend share with medium businesses and/or share with large businesses outside the USA

What you noted as the overall implication for ITC may be different to this - and in the realm of implications, there is no right answer.

What is however crucial is that your implications at each level always draw on information you have and that you are not selective in the information you draw on to get to your overall implications.

WRITING PYRAMIDS AS PROSE

Constructing a pyramid visually can be very helpful as you brainstorm what should go into your pyramid—the shape allows you to try different ways of laying out your thinking and helps with structuring your communication.

A pyramid can however get very big and cumbersome to document. I find it often works well to document the first tier of your pyramid visually—or if you have drawn it on a whiteboard, take a photo of it—and then document your full pyramid in prose.

To write a pyramid in prose, write each item of the pyramid as a separate bullet. To differentiate between the different levels of a pyramid, use different levels of indentation and different bullet shapes to indicate one level versus another.

For example, the pyramids in Figure 23 and Figure 24 which have two levels can be written using two levels of indent and two different style of bullets:

- Strategy in need of revision to encompass plans in services.
  - ITC's mission is to be the leading reseller and IT services provider in North America and Europe.
  - Its stated strategy, designed five years ago, focuses on being a reseller and not on services.

- Current projections fall short of three year profit target by $8m, with heavy reliance on USA for revenue and profit.
  - Revenue for the past year was $360m and has grown by 8% over the past three years.
  - Over the past three years, this comprises 23% growth with medium size business and 4% decline with large business.
  - 80% revenue and 85% profit from USA.
  - Overall profitability flat past three years, created by falling profits from large business and increasing profits from small business.
  - Projected profitability growth by segment is an average 1%, and 10% and 10% respectively per year, yielding profit of $42m in three years time.

If you include a third level—for example if you were to write the full pyramid for Figure 25 with three levels of prose—then you would need three levels of indents and three different style of bullets, as per the excerpt below:

- To meet $50m profit goal and close the $8m shortfall projected by our Corporate plan, ITC will need to both successfully win contract renewals and extend their range of services, and extend share with medium businesses and/or share with large businesses outside the USA.
  - Strategy in need of revision to encompass plans in services
    - ITC's mission is to be the leading reseller and IT services provider in North America and Europe
    - Its stated strategy, designed five years ago, focuses on being a reseller and not on services

And so on, until the full pyramid is written in prose, with appropriate indents and bullets.

CREATING YOUR D$_2$IAGNOSIS DOCUMENT

With your implications written down, you can now create your D$_2$iagnosis Document. You can do this by adding your implications to your completed dummy deck in one of two ways:

1. Putting the implications at the beginning of the document, followed by the findings that led to these, or
2. Putting the implications at the end, after the findings.

The best order for you will depend on your audience and on how surprising the implications are. For example, if the implications are contentious then you will likely want to put these after your findings, with the evidence first, to lead your audience towards your conclusions. However, If the implications are straightforward, you can put them upfront, which has the benefit starting with the most important messages.

Once you've decided which format you will use, create the slide(s) that synthesize the implications you have found, as per the example for ITC below. Spend time to make this punchy, if your audience remembers nothing else, you want them to remember these implications.

With your D$_2$iagnosis in place, you know your starting point and have alignment on it. From the first step D$_1$efine, you also know your goal and the key question and sub-questions you will need to address to get there. Now it is time to move into D$_3$evelop, exploring and testing hypotheses to go from the starting point identified by your D$_2$iagnosis to delivery of your goal.

Our diagnosis projects a shortfall of $8m to reach $50m profit target

To meet $50m profit goal and close the $8m shortfall projected by our Corporate plan, ITC will need to both successfully win contract renewals and extend their range of services, and extend share with medium businesses and/or share with large businesses outside the USA.

Other key findings are:
- Strategy in need of revision to encompass plans in services
- Current projections fall short of 3 year profit target by $8m
- Heavy reliance on USA for revenue and profit
- Reliance on 17 customers with more than half of this revenue up for tender next three years
- Opportunity to create modularized services offer
- Opportunity to extend existing end-of-life recycling offer
- Competitor success coming from focus on specific customer groups with targeted offerings.

D₂IAGNOSIS CHECKLIST

- You have rigorously gathered information to diagnose your situation without bias.

- The information is based on facts, and where this is not possible, a range of named interview sources.

- All sources of information are provided.

- You have mitigated for biases in how you have sought, reviewed and presented the information.

- You have structured your findings into a document.

- If you have used slides, you have one message per slide, expressed as the slide title, and supported by the information on the body of the slide.

- Your document is clearly and consistently formatted to avoid any distraction from the content.

- You have created a summary of your D₂iagnosis findings, drawing out implications and potentially using the Minto Pyramid Principle® to structure it.

- When you step back and read your D₂iagnosis synthesis, you are confident this provides a precise and objective D₂iagnosis of the situation that is fully based on your findings.

D_1efine

D_2iagnose

D_3evelop

D_4ecide

D_5eliver

3.1

GENERATE HYPOTHESES

"Nothing is easier than self-deceit. For what every man wishes, that he also believes to be true."

Demosthenes

Strategy in 5D

Step	Chapter	Actions
D$_1$efine	1.1 Define Your Goal	Articulate goal as question ↓ Brainstorm sub-questions
	1.2 Map Your Domain	Structure sub-questions
D$_2$iagnose	2.1 Diagnose Your Situation	Gather facts ↓ Draw insights ↓ Share findings
D$_3$evelop	3.1 Generate Hypotheses	Develop hypotheses ↓ Gather evidence
	3.2 Test Hypotheses	Repeat until hypotheses confirmed or disproved ↓ Draw insights ↓ Share findings
D$_4$ecide	4.1 Make Choices	Review combinations ↓ Debate scenarios
	4.2 Write Your Strategy	Document choices
D$_5$eliver	5.1 Communicate Your Strategy	Communicate strategy ↓ Pilot approach
	5.2 Deliver Results	Adapt approach ↓ Track progress

ARC at every step

KEY IDEAS

With your diagnosis in place, you are ready to begin the **D₃evelop** step and address sub-questions related to this step. You can do this by working through and answering each of the sub-questions individually or through generating hypotheses to cover the set of plausible answers to these sub-questions.

Using a hypothesis-driven approach means that you test your best working assumptions of the answer—your hypotheses—and revise these hypotheses according to the evidence you find until each hypothesis can either be confirmed true or discarded.

Working with such a set of hypotheses can save you a lot of time because it allows you to focus your information gathering activities solely on the evidence needed to prove or disprove your hypotheses.

A big note of caution: If you (or your key stakeholders) need an idea to be right once you have voiced it, do not use hypotheses. The hypothesis-driven approach only works if you are willing to be wrong and to discard your ideas in the light of new evidence. There is absolutely no place for dogmatism, nor sticking to a hypothesis regardless of whether the evidence supports it. If any of this is a concern, you are far better off answering each sub-question comprehensively and getting to the right answer a little more slowly, than you would be using a hypothesis-driven approach.

Your hypotheses need to address all the sub-questions relating to the **D₃evelop** step. Or in other words, your set of hypotheses cover the range of plausible answers to your D₃evelop sub-questions.

There is no need to generate hypotheses for other parts of the tree: You have already completed the **D₂iagnose** step, and if you wanted to use the hypothesis-driven approach for **D₄ecide** or **D₅eliver**, you would first have to have developed what your options are. You must, first complete the **D₃evelop** step, so you know what options you will be choosing from in **D₄ecide** and from there, what choices you will be implementing in **D₅eliver**.

Hypotheses are not facts. They need to be written in a form that is **specific, meaningful** and **testable**. Until proven, they are open to questioning and probing by all. Only a rigorous, continued refinement of your hypotheses, including at times totally discarding and replacing some of them, will lead to robust choices and ultimately a solid strategy. Don't let yourself be tempted into stating a hypothesis as a fact, no matter how confident you feel about it being right. If you don't yet have the evidence, it remains a hypothesis.

Your use of hypotheses may make colleagues nervous because they think that you have already decided what the answer is and that you are no longer open to alternatives. Look out for any signs of this and corral expectations. Clearly communicate your desire to understand the evidence, whatever it shows. Remind colleagues that you are not attached to the outcome or to a particular hypothesis being proven true—all that matters is what the evidence says. Demonstrate this mindset by being upfront when the evidence does not support one of your hypotheses, no matter how much the hypothesis may have been lauded previously.

DELIVERABLES, CONCEPTS, ARC AND MEETINGS

Step	Chapter	Key Concepts	Deliverables
D$_3$evelop	3.1 Generate Options	SMT (Specific, Measurable, Testable) hypotheses	D$_3$evelop Evidence Table

Examples of applying ARC to generating hypotheses are:

- Hypotheses are **actionable**, meaning they describe a concrete action that could be taken by the organization.
- Hypotheses are articulated with **rigor** and in a way that allows them to be tested.
- Hypotheses are generated **collaboratively** by the strategy design team and ideally with key stakeholders.

The key meetings required to complete this chapter are:

- Strategy design team:
  - Generate hypotheses via brainstorming session.

- Steering committee:
  - If you have stakeholders with the time and drive to roll up their sleeves, conduct a joint brainstorming session with the strategy design team. Alternatively, have a separate meeting with the key stakeholders as part of the testing and refinement process.

IDENTIFYING TOPICS FOR YOUR HYPOTHESES

Your hypotheses are your working assumptions of the best ways to address your **D$_3$evelop** sub-questions, given your D$_2$iagnosis from the previous chapter.

Hypotheses are the most viable options you can surmise. They are developed iteratively, starting with identifying topic areas for viable options. For example, if you surmise that "developing modularized services" is a viable option for addressing the growth required by your sub-questions, then this is a topic from which you need to develop a specific hypothesis.

The best way to develop your topic list and then your hypotheses is to take your **D$_3$evelop** sub-questions as a whole and list all viable options to answer them. Unlike the D$_2$iagnosis Information Table where each sub-question sits on its own row, since there is not a 1:1 relationship between sub-questions and hypotheses (there can be multiple hypotheses for one sub-question and one hypothesis for multiple sub-questions), it is important to list all the sub-questions as part of one row, and leaving space in the next column for all hypotheses, also all on the same row. This is show overleaf in the D$_3$evelop Evidence Table.[26]

D$_3$EVELOP EVIDENCE TABLE		
Diagnosis: To meet $50m profit goal ITC needs to successfully win contract renewals and extend range of services, and extend share with medium businesses and/or share with large businesses outside the US to meet $8m gap from corporate plan.		
Sub-questions	Hypothesis	Required Evidence
4.1 What opportunities are there to provide more of the current products and services to existing customers, and what could this deliver financially?		
4.2 Who and where are the most promising new customers to sell current products and services, and what could this deliver financially?		
4.3 What new products or services could ITC provide to meet the needs of existing customers, and what could this deliver financially?		
4.4 What new products or services could ITC provide to meet the needs of new customers, and what could this deliver financially?		
5.1 What cost reduction opportunities are there in how ITC serve the customer?		
5.2 What cost opportunities are there when rethinking how ITC support customer-facing work?		

Let's take sub-question 4.1 for ITC by way of example:

4. 1 What opportunities are there to provide more of the current products and services to existing customers, and what could this deliver financially?

We know from the **D₂iagnose** step that ITC is very focused on the US and so a potential option—and hence topic for a hypothesis— could be around expanding geographically. But is this the only topic you would have for 4.1? Probably not. For example, one competitor has successfully developed a webshop that has both grown business and reduced cost to serve. So there may be a hypothesis about developing a webshop.

You can already see that there can be multiple hypotheses per sub-question. One hypothesis can also relate to multiple sub-questions. For example, the idea of building an efficient webshop is not only relevant to growth with existing customers as per sub-question 4.1 but also cost reduction opportunities in how ITC serves its customers (sub-question 5.1).

This means that when generating hypotheses you need to be looking at your full list of **D₃evelop** sub-questions and from there, identify viable options that reach across each of them.

Involve all key stakeholders in generating the hypotheses, both to get their ideas and their buy-in. You can do this either by inviting them to brainstorm topics with you, or by providing them with a preliminary list of hypotheses as a basis for discussion.

If you are brainstorming as a team, it works best if you can generate options as a group and display all your relevant sub-questions on one side of a whiteboard. You don't need all tiers of your sub-questions, just those of the most detailed tier. Then on the other side of your whiteboard, start listing topics for your hypotheses, as per the example for ITC overleaf:

D₃evelop sub-questions

	Topics for hypotheses
4.1 What opportunities are there to provide more of the current products and services to existing customers, and what could this deliver financially	Geographical expansion
4.2 Who and where are the most promising new customers to sell current products and services, and what could this deliver financially?	Webshop
4.3 What new products or services could ITC provide to meet the needs of existing customers, and what could this deliver financially?	Recycling services
4.4 What new products or services could ITC provide to meet the needs of new customers, and what could this deliver financially?	Modularized services
5.1 What cost reduction opportunities are there in how ITC serve the customer?	New contracts
5.2 What cost opportunities are there when rethinking how ITC support customer-facing work?	Cost-savings share
	Slow-moving stock

Figure 26: Example list of topics for hypotheses from brainstorm

MOVING FROM TOPICS TO FULL HYPOTHESES

Now that you've identified your list of topics you need to develop them into hypotheses. That is, you write you possible options into statements that can then be tested.

Developing hypotheses is an iterative process and requires taking each topic area and articulating **specific** statement(s) of the most viable option(s) related to the topic. There is no point in claiming a topic as a hypotheses—such as "Expand overseas"—as topics are neither specific enough to be tested with evidence not able to be translated into tangible actions. By contrast "Double sales team in UK to triple UK profit by 2018" is specific and can be tested, and if proved true, is actionable.

Nor is there any point in hypotheses that don't provide a possible, relevant and **meaningful** option for the organization, even if they are specific. An example of an unmeaningful option for ITC would be "ITC has options to grow overseas given its strong dependence on the US market today". This doesn't tell us anything useful. It doesn't even tell us whether it would be a good option to grow overseas, it only tells us that there are options to do so.

Bear in mind also that each hypothesis needs to be tested with evidence and revised based on that evidence until such point as it can be proved or disproved. Thus, each hypothesis needs to be written in a way that makes it **testable** with evidence.

Take your list of topics and think through the statements of the most viable option(s) which are **specific, meaningful** and **testable** (**SMT**).

Don't expect to write your hypotheses in a specific, meaningful and testable way straight off. Typically you will need to translate your topic into a statement and then rewrite your statement several times until you have a **specific, meaningful** and **testable** hypothesis.

Topics for hypotheses   Refinement towards hypotheses

Geographical expansion

- ~~Double UK sales team to triple profit~~
- ~~Build out in China~~
- Expand in Canada and Continental Europe to grow profit per country by 50%

Webshop

- ~~Replace existing shopping section of website with shopping section~~
- ~~Build out existing website~~
- Create new, separate, user-friendly webshop

Recycling services

- ~~Develop bespoke recycling services for European customers~~
- ~~Create cradle to grave recycling services for US~~
- Extend existing end-of-life recycling offer

Modularized services

- ~~Develop modularized services for largest customers~~
- ~~Review existing services and modularize top 3~~
- Create full à la carte menu of modularized services, particularly for small and medium-sized businesses

New contracts

- ~~Win 10 new contracts in 2017~~
- ~~Win 2 new contracts in telco sector~~
- Win three new large contracts of at least $100m each

Cost-savings share

- ~~Set up cost-savings share model for customers of at least five years~~
- Set up cost-savings model available to all managed services customers

Slow-moving stock

- ~~Sell slow moving stock in Europe~~
- Sell stock once it gets to 90 days rather than today's 120 days

Figure 27: Example refinement towards hypotheses

As you add depth and detail to your hypothesis, follow the practice of writing out in full each articulation of hypothesis so everyone can see it and comment on the wording to ensure it is precise. You may also need to take a pause and sleep on your interim hypotheses before returning to them to make sure that they are **specific**, **meaningful** and **testable** (SMT). You can do this by applying the questions below to each hypothesis:

S pecific
- Is the hypothesis clear?
- Does it make sense on a stand-alone basis?

M eaningful
- Is it relevant?
- Does it matter whether it is true or not?
- If it were true, would it give rise to a tangible decision?

T estable
- Is it written in a way that allows for it to be proved or disproved by evidence?
- If not, can it be rewritten, for example by being broken down into testable components?
- Is there a counterexample which could refute the hypothesis? (There should be one if there hypothesis is truly testable)

Overleaf are a few examples of poorly written hypotheses that do not fulfill the SMT criteria and how each could be improved to make them specific, meaningful and testable:

Example 1

Original hypothesis	Recycling regulation is increasing
Verdict	Not specific. A rather sweeping statement—does it apply to all products and all customers?
Better hypothesis	Extend existing end-of-life recycling offer to add 3% to revenue and profit.

Example 2

Original hypothesis	ITC can improve marketing of international capabilities.
Verdict	Not meaningful. Doesn't really tell us anything and certainly not the potential impact of this initiative.
Better hypothesis	Improve marketing of overseas capabilities to US companies with overseas presence to increase business in Canada, UK and Germany by 50%.

Example 3

Original hypothesis	There are 101,645 organizations worldwide who would want to buy ITC's modularized services.
Verdict	Not testable. Too precise to be realistically testable. If you could find 101,646 organizations worldwide who wanted ITC's modular services, then you would have tested and disproved this hypothesis. But this is not a realistic amount of work.
Better hypothesis	The market potential for modularized services in the US is at least 100 organizations. (Market potential may be much more, but we only need to know there is sufficient interest, here taken as at least 100 organizations, to support development of the proposition).

Review the following four hypotheses. Are they specific, meaningful and testable (SMT)? Please note down your thoughts:

1. Our customers can be segmented.

_____

_____

_____

2. We should focus on customers who are looking for a low cost offering to improve their profitability.

_____

_____

_____

3. Our primary customer base needs a high-quality, efficient service and is prepared to pay a premium for it.

_____

_____

_____

4. Revenue growth is important to restore ITC's profitability.

_____

_____

_____

Please see the Appendix, on page 317, for comments on each of these.

REVIEWING YOUR HYPOTHESES

Unlike the sub-questions in your D$_1$efine Question Tree, that need to be MECE, your hypotheses don't need to cover every possible tenet and subset, in fact it would be incredibly difficult, if not impossible, to do this. Your hypotheses do, however, need to address all key and likely components of your solution.

Beware of creating too many hypotheses that are effectively testing a copy of what a competitor is doing. By all means there may be an opportunity to do something similar but better. For example, lower price, better service or enhanced features. Simply doing the same, however, creates no competitive advantage. Back to *Moneyball:* as Billy Bean, the manager of the Oakland A's says regarding discussions in the boardroom about which players to buy, "If we try to play like the Yankees in here, we will lose to the Yankees out there."

At this stage, you want to generate more hypotheses than will ultimately make up your strategy, so don't limit yourself too early. Give yourself and your stakeholders enough material to make meaningful choices at a later stage.

USING HYPOTHESES AS A WAY TO PRIORITIZE

Hypotheses can provide a way to prioritize the work to be done. Often when you review your full set of hypotheses you can identify two or three hypotheses that are pivotal to the direction of the answer to the overall question.

Taking ITC's overall question as an example, you are looking for the best actions ITC can take to develop capabilities and achieve sustainable profit of at least $50m per year from 2018. That means a pivotal line of enquiry—unless this has already been closed off during the diagnosis—is to confirm whether this can come through cost reduction or must come primarily or even solely through revenue growth.

A starting point would be to assert a hypothesis on whether cost reductions can or cannot meet the profitability goal, for example:

- Cost reductions could save 25% of current cost base, sufficient to restore profitability, or
- Cost reductions could at most total 10% of cost base whereas a minimum of 25% would be required to restore profitability.

With either hypothesis, the evidence you want is the same:

a. Calculation of the level of cost reductions required to restore profitability within three years; and
b. Review of costs by category including what level of cost reductions would be possible.

This evidence would then either prove or disprove the hypotheses above. This also cues up the next hypothesis to be tested. In this example, either cost will have been shown to be insufficient to restore profitability and revenue growth hypotheses must be tested, or cost reductions are sufficient and further hypotheses need to be tested on what to cut and how best to do it.

CONFIRMING HYPOTHESES ARE TESTABLE

A good way to check that each hypothesis is testable is to identify evidence to test it with. Let's return to our three "better hypotheses" identified earlier in this chapter, mapping out columns two and three of the D_3evelop Evidence Table.

In the example overleaf, all the hypotheses have the evidence to be testable. If this were not the case, then you'd need to rethink whether there are other ways to formulate each hypothesis to make them testable or whether to ask for input from stakeholders for possible evidence.

| D₃EVELOP EVIDENCE TABLE (EXCERPT) ||
Hypothesis	Required Evidence
Extend existing end-of-life recycling offer to add 3% to revenue and profit	• Services design team to spec out what extended services would be and their cost • Test with existing customers • Confirm financial potential based on feedback
Grow profit in Canada, UK and Germany by 50% by marketing overseas capabilities to US customers	• Understand from existing US customers: – Their satisfaction – Their needs outside US – How those needs are serviced today – Interest in ITC providing those services
The market potential for modularized services in the US is at least 100 organizations	• Identify the number of organizations in target market • Mock-up what modularized services would provide • Talk to at least 20 customers to test for interest in modularized services • Review competitor success with modularized services • Extrapolate customer interest and competitor success to test if at least 100 organizations interested

EXERCISE: PLAYING DEVIL'S ADVOCATE

A fun exercise and one that can have great impact is to take the exact opposite of each of your hypotheses and try to find evidence to prove them. You can do this alone or, even better, with a group of stakeholders who have strong views on the hypotheses.

Divide stakeholders into smaller groups and assign a hypothesis to each group, ideally where at least some of the group agree with it and some do not. Ask for evidence to support the opposite hypothesis and for this to be presented to all.

This can have stunning results, as it cuts out "my idea" versus "your idea" fueled discussions, which can get mired in emotions. Instead, the focus is on proving hypotheses solely through evidence. This first-hand experience of arguing the opposite of your hypothesis is especially powerful for individuals with entrenched viewpoints.

KEY CONCEPT: THE ROLE OF INTUITION

I am often asked if the analytical techniques I teach preclude intuition. Absolutely not. The best problem solvers combine their intuition and gut feeling with a strong reliance on evidence and analysis.

Generating solid hypotheses can draw heavily on your intuition and feeling for the answers to the problem. So don't hold back on using your intuition. The best senior manager I have worked with had an amazing commercial gut feel for what products and services would work, and what customers and suppliers needed. Yet, he was always open to evidence and facts to the contrary and in fact was grateful when these were brought to his attention so that he had a full view before making a decision.

DOCUMENTING YOUR HYPOTHESES

You can use the **D$_3$evelop Evidence Table** introduced earlier in the chapter to document your hypotheses and the evidence required to test them. It is analogous to the D$_2$iagnosis Information Table you used in the previous chapter, although given the complexity and iterative nature of the findings in this step, we use two tables as part of D$_3$eveloping—the D$_3$evelop Evidence Table to document what your are looking for and then, in the next chapter, D$_3$evelop Findings Tables, which contain your findings documented by hypothesis.

As discussed earlier, when we compiled our topics, hypotheses do not map 1-to-1 to sub-questions. That is, one hypothesis can relate to several sub-questions and several hypotheses can relate to one sub-question.

The list of evidence you include needs to be sufficient to know that the hypothesis is testable. At this stage, this list of evidence is unlikely to be the full and final list you need, as these requirements will change as you gather and review evidence and as your thinking develops. What matters is that you list evidence which will test your hypotheses.

Also included in the D$_3$evelop Evidence Table for ITC is:

- A recap of the diagnosis (at the top of the table).
- Estimated financial impact of all the hypotheses (in the Hypotheses column under a description of the hypothesis).
- Source(s) for each piece of evidence (these are included in the way the evidence is articulated in the Required Evidence e.g. test options with customers for feedback, where customers are the source. You could alternatively add to the table an additional column for your sources).
- Owner and timing for each hypothesis (included in the Required Evidence column although you could create a separate column for these too).

D₃EVELOP EVIDENCE TABLE		
Diagnosis: To meet $50m profit goal ITC needs to successfully win contract renewals and extend range of services, and extend share with medium businesses and/or share with large businesses outside the US to meet $8m gap from corporate plan.		
Sub-questions	Hypothesis	Required Evidence
4.1 What opportunities are there to provide more of the current products and services to existing customers, and what could this deliver financially?	**A. Overseas sales teams** Grow profit in Canada, UK and Germany by 50% by marketing overseas capabilities to US customers (estimated profit per year = profit outside US x 50% = 15% x $35m x 50% = $2.6m, less costs to be calculated)	• Understand from existing US customers: - Their satisfaction - Their needs outside US - How those needs are serviced today - Interest in ITC providing those services *Tyler Feb 1st*
4.2 Who and where are the most promising new customers to sell current products and services, and what could this deliver financially?	**B. Cost-savings share** For managed services customers, create a cost-savings share model (estimated profit per year of $0.5m based on $100k profit per customer and five customers)	• Brainstorm options for how this could work • Test options with customers for feedback *Saffron* *Feb 1st*

D₃EVELOP EVIDENCE TABLE		
4.3 What new products or services could ITC provide to meet the needs of existing customers, and what could this deliver financially?	**C. Recycling** Extend existing end-of-life recycling offer to add 3% to revenue and profit ($1m additional profit based on average add to each customer)	• Propositions team to spec out what new services would be and their cost • Test with existing customers *Lydia* *Feb 1st*
	D. New contracts Win three new contracts in next three years of at least $100m (min $3m profit per year as $1m each)	• Identify shortlist of possible new contracts • Confirm financial potential based on feedback *Saffron* *Feb 1st*
4.4 What new products or services could ITC provide to meet the needs of new customers, and what could this deliver financially? 5.1 What cost reduction opportunities are there in how ITC serve the customer?	**E. Modularized Services** Create a modularized services offer, with flexible à la carte choice of services to increase US market share by 1% in each of small and medium business markets (worth $3.25m additional profit)	• Proposition team to craft options for offer • Test with existing and potential customers *James* *Feb 1st*

D₃EVELOP EVIDENCE TABLE		
5.2 What cost opportunities are there when rethinking how ITC support customer-facing work?	**F. Webshop** Create a robust webshop to increase sales by 10% and run 50% product business through it (save $1m per year, with $2m upfront investment)	• Analyze impact of competitor webshops • Test mock-up with customers *Lydia* *Feb 8th*
	G. Slow-moving stock Sell off slow moving stock effectively after 90 days (saves $1m per year)	• Develop and test cost projections with finance team *Tyler* *Feb 8th*
Estimated impact to profit = $12.4m per year Suggests hypotheses could deliver the required additional $8m profit per year; all now needs testing		

REVIEWING YOUR HYPOTHESES

With your D₃evelop Evidence Table complete, step back and check four things:

1. Is every hypothesis specific, meaningful and testable (SMT)?
2. Could these hypotheses provide a set of choices from which to form a strategy?
3. Is anything missing from this set of choices?
4. Does the estimated financial impact meet the overall goal?

In the instance where 4. is not met and the estimated impact of the hypotheses is insufficient to meet the overall goal, then look to see if there are further legitimate hypotheses to add. If this is not the case, then you should highlight the potential shortfall to the steering committee, pending full findings from the hypothesis testing phase (i.e. it could change helpfully toward your financial goal or unhelpfully away from is, depending on the evidence uncovered.)

Once you are comfortable that you have a robust set of hypotheses you can add the D_3evelop Evidence Table (in Word or pasted from Excel) to the *Discovery Document* and prepare to test your hypotheses.

D$_3$EVELOPING HYPOTHESES CHECKLIST

- You have a set of hypotheses that cover all your plausible options.

- Each hypothesis is specific and makes sense on its own.

- Each hypothesis is meaningful.

- Each hypothesis is testable.

- You continually evolve the hypotheses in the light of evidence.

- You are willing at any time to discard a hypothesis which evidence does not support.

- You engage key stakeholders in generating hypotheses, or if not, at least in reviewing suggested hypotheses.

3.2

TEST HYPOTHESES

"I had, also, during many years followed a golden rule, namely, that whenever a published fact, a new observation or thought came across me, which was opposed to my general results, to make a memorandum of it without fail and at once; for I had found by experience that such facts and thoughts were far more apt to escape from the memory than favorable ones."

Charles Darwin

Strategy in 5D		
Step	**Chapter**	**Actions**
D₁efine	1.1 Define Your Goal	Articulate goal as question ↓ Brainstorm sub-questions
	1.2 Map Your Domain	Structure sub-questions
D₂iagnose	2.1 Diagnose Your Situation	Gather facts ↓ Draw insights ↓ Share findings
D₃evelop	3.1 Generate Hypotheses	Develop hypotheses
		Gather evidence ←
		Repeat until hypotheses confirmed or disproved
	3.2 Test Hypotheses	
		Draw insights
		Share findings
D₄ecide	4.1 Make Choices	Review combinations ↓ Debate scenarios
	4.2 Write Your Strategy	Document choices
D₅eliver	5.1 Communicate Your Strategy	Communicate strategy ↓ Pilot approach
	5.2 Deliver Results	Adapt approach ↓ Track progress
ARC at every step		

KEY IDEAS

You are now entering a phase of testing your hypotheses with evidence. You will likely have to go through several iterations of gathering evidence, reviewing it, revising your hypotheses and gathering and reviewing more evidence until you can either prove or disprove each hypothesis.

I affectionately call this the "washing machine phase" with each hypothesis being turned over and over, adding evidence as a sort of washing powder that cleans up each hypothesis. If, after multiple washing cycles with fresh washing powder (evidence), your hypothesis still does not come out clean (the evidence does not prove it), then discard it and move forward only with the clean ones. Figure 28 depicts this phase showing how with each iteration you end up with a rejected hypothesis, a confirmed hypothesis or a revised hypothesis to test.

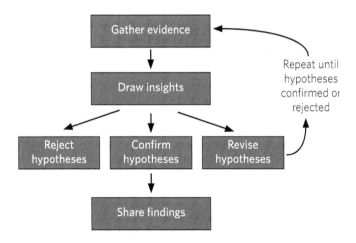

Figure 28: Hypotheses-driven approach: the "washing machine phase"

Do not underestimate the time and rigor required for the hypothesis testing phase, to ensure you test each hypothesis in an unbiased way.

Uncovering new information is rarely a linear process and it requires navigation and stamina. Multiple iterations and cycles of the washing machine help refine the richness and accuracy of your evidence, and as you inevitably discover some evidence you didn't expect, not only will your hypotheses need to be refined, you will also identify new evidence that then needs to be gathered.

Your starting point is to confirm that you have identified the evidence you need in order to prove, or disprove each hypothesis. Be precise and creative here: where are the best places to get the evidence you need? Who are the best people to talk to? Thinking laterally can help you gather a lot of valuable but harder to find information. Think of it as detective work.

You are likely to want to conduct:

1. **Desk-based research**, including insights from reports, interviews, quotes and numbers.
2. **Interviews** with customers, competitors, market experts and staff, amongst others.

For each hypothesis, there are often two or three key pieces of evidence that prove or disprove it. At times you can identify these upfront. Other times you may gather a lot of evidence and then as you review the evidence realize that a couple of pieces alone will determine whether the hypothesis is true.

This is consistent with adopting an 80:20 approach, also known as Pareto's law. It states that 80% of the results come from 20% of the effort, so focus on the 20% of effort that will yield the most critical evidence.

For each and every piece of evidence you want to understand how reliable it is. Bear this in mind as you gather evidence—it may lead you to discard certain sources as less reliable or decide to gather information from a larger variety of sources even during the initial evidence gathering phase. You will inevitably end up discarding pieces of evidence because their source is not reliable enough or because you can find more robust evidence. Just be sure to document why you didn't use a piece of evidence as this can be an invaluable record when someone asks you months down the track.

You then want to ask, "What is the evidence telling me?" Put aside your preconceptions and strive to see the evidence for what it is.

Having an open and curious mind and really wanting to know the truth will serve you well here. The analysis of evidence needs to go beyond summarizing the information and draw out the implications it brings with it. For instance, alone three pieces of data may say three separate things but when analyzed together they may provide insights well beyond those provided individually.

From the moment you start to gather and review your findings, document them as well. Take the time to structure your findings, update your hypotheses and identify any new information that is required. In this chapter we introduce D_3evelop Findings Tables which provide a structure for capturing the findings for each hypothesis. This will pay dividends in terms of the clarity of your own thinking and will provide a way to communicate progress to stakeholders. It also helps you sort through information and not get stuck on some detail at the expense of all the other pieces of information required.

Just as you did with the diagnosis, you want to identify how you will capture and display the evidence. The more you can define your end product upfront, the more precise you can be in identifying the exact evidence you need—and don't need—thus making the most efficient use of your time.

As you move towards your final cycles of the washing machine, every hypothesis you started with needs to become either proved or disproved—since no matter how many time your hypothesis is revised at some point you need to conclude that can be proved or not.

Once you have worked each original hypothesis through to being provided or disproved you have a list of confirmed options, and of those which were rejected—your D$_4$evelop Conclusions Table.

Include in this table the estimated financial impact of each confirmed option. Then step back and look at the table to determine if, collectively, you have sufficient options to meet the goal expressed in your overall question. There are three possibilities:

1. Considered collectively, the estimated impact of all your possible options is insufficient to meet your goal. Unless there are any genuine and plausible hypotheses that you did not test in this step D$_3$evelop—and do not try to find any reasons to reintroduce a hypothesis that you have already legitimately ruled out—then it is best to meet with stakeholders and discuss these findings and as a result, whether your original goal is unrealistic and needs to be revised
2. Considered collectively, the estimated impact of your options is just sufficient to meet your goal. Provided it is practical, you are likely to want to pursue all these possible options, albeit sequenced to ensure sufficient focus on each for success. More on this in the next chapter.
3. Considered collectively, the estimated impact of your possible options is more than sufficient to meet your goal. Your task then is to decide which of these to pursue—more of this in the next chapter and step D$_4$ecide.

The **D$_3$evelop** step of Strategy in 5D and specifically this component of hypothesis testing is the most time consuming of the first four steps. You want to spell out upfront that this will take several weeks (in a ten week process typically no fewer than four) and schedule a set of meetings at least once a week where findings are discussed. Given the likely duration and intensity of this phase, it is particularly important here to structure the work and agree on activities, responsibilities and due dates with the strategy design team to ensure everyone is on board.

DELIVERABLES, CONCEPTS, ARC AND MEETINGS

Step	Chapter	Key Concepts	Deliverables
D₃evelop	3.2 Test Hypotheses	Estimates grid Summary versus Synthesis "So whats" 80:20 rule (Pareto's Law) Prioritization matrix	D₃evelop Findings Tables D₃evelop Conclusion Table

Examples of applying ARC for testing your hypotheses are:

Evidence

- Evidence required is **actionable**, meaning the evidence exists and can be obtained.
- Evidence is fairly and **rigorously** obtained from a wide range of sources.
- Strategy design team **collaborate** to compile a list of evidence and this list is shared for input. Stakeholders are engaged in instances where cannot identify evidence and want their input on possible sources.

Findings

- Revisions to the hypotheses ensure that they continue to be **actionable**.
- Findings are discussed **collaboratively**, with regularity and openness (no concealing of any information).
- Interpretation of evidence is **rigorous** and mitigated for cognitive biases.
- *Discovery Document* is **rigorously** updated to include findings, latest formulation of hypotheses and further information sought.
- Revisions to hypotheses are fair and **rigorous**, based on full review of evidence found.

The key meetings required to complete this chapter are:

- Strategy design team:
  - Initial meeting to review list of evidence and agree responsibilities. Twice-weekly meetings to share and review findings, reformulate hypotheses and ensure clarity on evidence still required.
- Steering committee:
  - Weekly or bi-weekly meetings to share and review findings. Review implications of hypothesis revisions and list of confirmed and rejected hypotheses.

REVIEWING REQUIRED EVIDENCE

Begin by reviewing the required evidence list you compiled in the D_3evelop Evidence Table. All your hypotheses should be testable. If there are any gaps in evidence, make an explicit note so you can get input from stakeholders and, where needed, return to identifying possible evidence as your thinking develops.

Consider the usefulness of each piece of evidence to avoid doing superfluous work. What insights could it provide? You may want to create a dummy deck to capture and structure findings, just as we did for the D_2iagnosis. If so, follow the same approach as in chapter 2.1, creating dummy titles for the slides and listing in the body of the slide the likely evidence to support the title. Here your hypotheses will form the titles of your slides and placed in the body will be the evidence that ultimately proves or disproves your hypothesis. Since your hypotheses will be revised several times, so will your dummy slides, reflecting the revisions to your hypotheses in the light of new evidence.

GATHERING EVIDENCE

For each hypothesis, consider what **desk-based research** you could do to prove or disprove it, for example:

- Are there reports written or numbers available that would provide quantitative evidence?
- Are there published interviews with experts relevant to your hypotheses?

Get input from colleagues by asking them what evidence they would seek if they were in your shoes.

Desk-based research provides both standalone pieces of evidence and a base for further exploration in interviews. There is no need to limit yourself to using your research to inform interviews that you have already decided on—let it inform your choice of interviewees. Suppose you have found a helpful research paper, can you talk to the author and ask them to suggest further reading materials? Better yet, ask the author to point out an opposing opinion so that you can explore that with equal rigor.

As you gather your desk-based research, be meticulous in documenting all your sources and creating well-structured files of documents. At the time you might remember the source of each piece of evidence, but as you gather more evidence you will find it increasingly difficult to remember where each has come from.

Interviews can provide richness and allow exploration and testing of a range of ideas and hypotheses that can complement your desk-based research. New ideas, perspectives and lines of enquiry often arise when talking to others and quotes from interviews can be enormously powerful. Interviews may also provide the only evidence you can get in an area that is not data-rich.

Make sure you have a broad range of people to interview who represent different views, including customers, employees suppliers, competitors (often easier if conducted by an outside independent party) and industry experts. Those who are not experts and who may see things from a different perspective can also open new windows of possibilities for you to investigate. If you can find the right mix of people and organizations to interview you will start to see a web of information forming that will push you forward exponentially in your search for answers.

With so much information available on the internet, most data and information gathering does not need to be requested in advance. This is not the case for interviews, which tend to have a lead time of a week or two to schedule time in people's calendars. As a result, it is best to set up interviews early and then use the time prior to the interviews to continue your desk-based research.

For anyone who feels a bit shy speaking to experts, there is no need to be. Most people would be delighted to hear that you have read their work and would love to talk to you about it.

At the time of requesting the interview, you don't need to know in precise detail what the interview will cover, just briefy explain the reason for the meeting and the major themes you want to discuss.

For example, if you were requesting an interview with one of ITC's customers to test the hypotheses, you could say:

"In response to your feedback, and that of other customers, we are looking to enhance our range of services, both in the US and possibly overseas.

Would you be willing to meet for an hour so we can learn what else ITC could provide you with to meet your future business needs and to test some early ideas we have for extending our services?"

In some cases it can also help to provide a list of the questions you intend to ask, so as to give interviewees the specifics to prepare. You don't need to provide these at the time you schedule the interview, but if you are going to do this make sure you provide them in time for the interviewee to prepare.

KEY CONCEPT: GOOD INTERVIEW PRACTICE

Good interview practice is imperative to getting the most out of each interview.

Prior to the interview:

- **Write down your objectives:** What is it you want from the interviews? What information do you need or what hypotheses are you testing? Ask yourself: "If this interview is successful what will I learn?" You do not want to leave the interview without having asked for what you need.

- **Consider whether one or two interviewers is best:** Two interviewers enables one to lead and the other to write notes, clarify the interviewee's answers and ask additional questions. One interviewer works best in a sensitive situation where the intimacy created can lead to a deeper and more frank conversation.

- **Research the person you are meeting:** Even if you know them, be sure to understand their background and their relationship to your organization.

- **Put yourself in the interviewee's shoes:** Will they want detailed questions in advance? What might their perspective be? What might their concerns be?

- **Draft an interview guide:** This lays out the hypotheses you want to test and the questions you will use to do so. Include who will be doing the interview and give context for what you are doing.

- **Craft open questions:** Also allocate time for new and unexpected information to arise. Be sure the questions you write are not leading ones or have a cognitive bias. For example, you may share a hypothesis and then ask what evidence they have seen to support or refute it.

- **Seek input on the interview guide:** This not only enables stakeholders to add questions you may have missed and to challenge you on cognitive biases, but also gets their buy-in. You definitely do not want to conduct a set of interviews only for your stakeholders to later tell you that you missed some crucial questions, or worse, reject the findings due to their discomfort with the interview guide.

- **Send details of the interview to interviewee:** Include the purpose, what to expect (and possibly the questions), plus location and timing. You may also want to reconfirm the interview the day before.

During the interview:

- **Give a proper introduction:** Provide background about yourself, your objectives, and how the interview will work. Also discuss what feedback they may want from the interviews. For example, would they like to hear the overall findings once interviews are done? Give time for the interviewee to introduce him/herself (if you have not met before) and ask any questions about the interview.

- **Be clear how you will use the interviewee's comments:** Establish with your interviewee beforehand whether they want their comments to be attributable or non-attributable. That is, whether you can refer to them in your overall findings or whether they would prefer to remain anonymous. You may also want to offer to share the overall results with them once the interviews are completed and if so, to agree how they would like that to occur e.g. in person, by phone, via email.

- **Use your interview guide as a guide, not a rigid structure:** Cover all key questions, but you do not need to do this in the order of your guide. What's more important is to follow the flow of the conversation. Inevitably you will want to, and should, ask additional or follow-up questions that are not on your guide. (Occasionally these are so good, you will want to add them to your guide for future interviews).

- **Remain aware of cognitive biases:** Keep questions open, listening for cognitive biases in the interviewee's responses, as well as in your own discourse.

- **Recap at key points:** Make sure you have understood the interviewee correctly. This also enables the interviewee to clarify or add detail to their earlier response.

- **Ask if it's okay to follow-up post interview:** You may think of additional questions or generate new hypotheses to test post interview. Leave the door open in case as you write up the notes, something needs clarification.

- **Request introductions to other interviewees, as needed:** The interviewee may be able to introduce you to other interviewees, especially once they have direct experience of what you are looking for.

After the interview:

Write-up interview notes: Be sure to take good notes and write them out while the interview is still fresh in your mind, within 48 hours. This may seem like a pain, but writing them helps crystallize and clarify what was said and identifies gaps for further exploration.

Say thank you: Write a thank you note. Showing gratitude helps keep the door open should you need to ask follow-up questions.

ADDRESSING EVIDENCE GAPS

Where you have gaps in your evidence, the following two approaches can be invaluable:

1. **Making estimates**
2. Asking **what you would need to believe for X** to be true (where X may be a piece of evidence or a component of the hypothesis).

The ability to **make estimates** underpinned by well-founded assumptions can cut through a hypothesis that is proving difficult to test.

Let's take an example. Suppose to test one of your hypotheses you need to know the annual demand for golf balls in the US. The key thing here is to be able to break this down into smaller components and make estimates from there. It works best if you identify:

- The inputs you are using to get to your answer.
- The sources you are using for each input

ESTIMATES GRID	
Inputs	**Source**
1. Population of US	US census
2. Proportion of population who play golf	Search online for estimates of % of adults in US who play golf
3. Average number of golf balls purchased per player per year	Search online for information about the average number of golf balls used per player per year Call a few golf stores or golf clubs and ask their opinion
From here you can take: 1.x2.x3. = estimate of number of golf balls sold in US annually	

Figure 29: Example Estimates Grid

By making your inputs and sources transparent, people can understand your thought process. It is helpful if you can check your estimates by finding more than one way of making the estimate (also known as triangulating). For example, with finding out the number of golf facilities in the US, you could then research the average number of players per facility and then an estimate of the number of balls purchased per player per year. If they have questions or don't agree with the estimate, they can discuss this with you at the level of assumptions, rather than through the numbers alone, which can often be emotive, and lacking in the details of how you got there.

If you are struggling to identify evidence then a second excellent approach is to ask yourself the question:

What would I need to believe for X to be true?

Let's take a couple of examples:

Example 1: Our business should invest in higher quality customer services.

As a business, for this to be true we would need to believe that investing in higher quality customer services would ultimately bring in more money.

To test if this were true, we would need to understand:

- What different levels of investment would mean for the quality of customer services.
- What the expected impact would be on customers and how they might behave differently as a result.
- Whether quality of customer service in the past was better or worse and how this affected income.
- Where you have colleagues who have worked for a competitor, how their customer services compare.

We would also want to consider the opportunity cost of this investment including:

- What's the cost/range for costs and options for upgrading customer services?
- What will be required to deliver it?
- How how easy or difficult is it to do?
- What are reasons to do it now rather than as a later point?
- What else could we do if we did not do this?

It is important when making estimates to remember cognitive biases and in particular sunk cost bias.

Suppose there is already a plan and lots of support from staff to make an investment in higher quality customer services, should this be a factor in the decision? No. The question remains whether a higher quality customer service would create more profit. Yet, if you are emotionally invested in this option, you can see just how easy it would be to argue it with "We can't stop now, otherwise employee motivation and what we've already achieved will be lost." Ask yourself, what decision would you make if you had not invested anything yet?

Example 2: We should expand our nonprofit's services from college scholarships to include job seeking and employment support.

To believe the above hypothesis to be true, we would want to know:

- That job seeking and employment support are services that are required by our users. (Could ascertain this from the staff who most work with users, or through conversations or polls with users.)
- There is no other nonprofit or other organization who is better placed to provide these services. (Would need to profile skills and services provided by other organizations in similar domain.)
- That our nonprofit has the right foundations to build these skills. (Could map current skills, skills required and any gaps that would need to be addressed.)

- That this is a more worthwhile opportunity than others our nonprofit could pursue. (Here could map all other possible opportunities and quickly evaluate along two dimensions: (1) Likely impact and (2) Ease of implementation. A good way to compare them is by plotting them on a prioritization matrix, like that below:

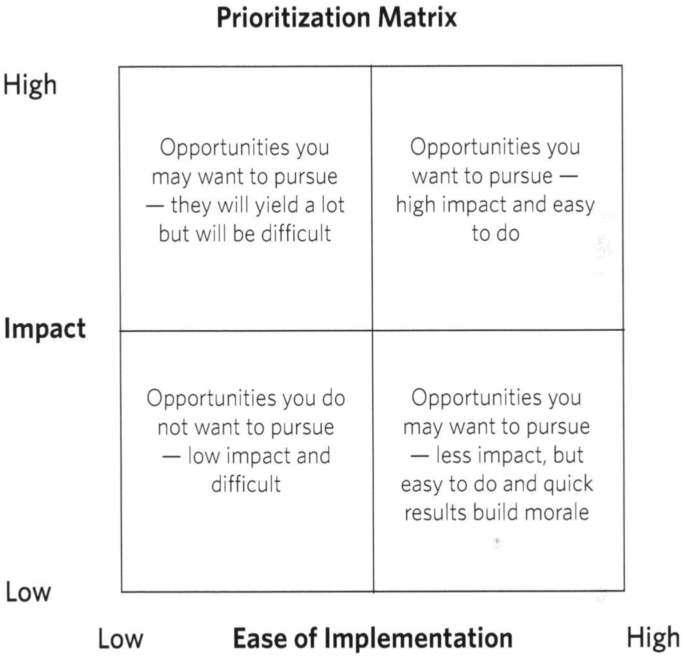

Prioritization Matrix

	Low Ease of Implementation	High
High	Opportunities you may want to pursue — they will yield a lot but will be difficult	Opportunities you want to pursue — high impact and easy to do
Impact		
Low	Opportunities you do not want to pursue — low impact and difficult	Opportunities you may want to pursue — less impact, but easy to do and quick results build morale

Low   **Ease of Implementation**   High

Figure 30: Matrix to prioritize opportunities by impact and ease

---

KEY CONCEPT: BEWARE OF CONFIRMATION BIAS

Stay alert for your own confirmation bias at all times during the hypothesis testing process, and acknowledge that your judgment can be easily clouded by it.

Play devil's advocate and explore what you would need to believe for the opposite of your hypothesis to be true. Seek evidence that would prove its opposite.

Avoid having a default position on anything.

Talk to people who have different views and seek to understand their views. Suppose you take the opposite viewpoint to your hypothesis, what would you have to believe for it to be true?

INTERPRETING YOUR EVIDENCE

The interpretation of your evidence is a crucial task that shapes your whole strategy through its impact on ultimately confirming or disproving your hypotheses.

You need to be very thorough in your treatment of each piece of evidence. This is not a simple box-checking exercise where you get the evidence and you are done regardless of what it says. Question it. Perhaps the data does not tell you what you expected it to, but see it for what it is.

Always perform a sanity check on your data. If the evidence looks wrong, then it probably is. If you have any doubts at all, review the evidence and any assumptions again. For example, if according to your calculations the annual demand for golf balls in the US comes out at 60bn (i.e. 200 balls per person), ask yourself if this seems sensible or if there is a mistake somewhere.

Put WYSIATI into practice by not half glancing at your evidence and assuming it says what you were expecting. What does it really say? Does it really prove or disprove your hypothesis? Perhaps, it suggests that the hypothesis needs to be revised and then tested further. Or does it provide a final piece of evidence that confirms a hypothesis?

Don't be afraid to discard evidence. You don't need to show all the evidence you have gathered. Resist wanting to show how much work you have done and instead focus on communicating your most striking findings. You will want to discard—or place in an appendix—evidence that is not robust or evidence that becomes superfluous due to better evidence.

Above all, be honest about what the evidence is telling you, and don't allow yourself to make assumptions on scanty or conflicting evidence or allow cognitive biases to mask the true meaning of the evidence.

EXAMPLE: INTERPRETING EVIDENCE

Let's return to Example 1 earlier in this chapter, the hypothesis that it is worth investing in higher quality customer service.

Suppose that the customer interviews reveal that customers are happy with the service they are receiving. Indeed, on average they rank the service they receive as better than that of competitors. Suppose also that during the interviews several customers raise an issue they are experiencing with one of your products and initial feedback suggests that this is losing you money. Report back to your stakeholders what you have heard and that there is no evidence to support the hypothesis.

Then ask that your effort can be pivoted to investigate the product issue that customers are highlighting to determine what actions should be taken.

DETERMINING IMPLICATIONS

With your evidence gathered and interpretation underway, you want to push yourself to determine what the evidence really means. One approach is to quickly write down all the key insights from your gathered evidence and then test and rewrite them into punchy lists of insights. McKinsey & Co refers to these as "so whats". Or in other words, "What are the implications of what you have found?"

KEY CONCEPT: SUMMARY VS SYNTHESIS

McKinsey consultants typically ask themselves and their team "so what?" dozens of times a day as they sort through a myriad of data and evidence.

A "so what" provides insights and inferences. It draws out the implications of the evidence into a new insight—a synthesis not a summary.

Summary = grouping of facts and information	Synthesis = "so whats" arising from the information
Needs of customers vary; some are common, some not	Customer needs are not homogeneous, can be divided into four groupings
Using computing language R provides control	By not using computing language R, we miss out on time savings, faster response and a greater range of experiments
New landing pages are making a difference	New landing pages are adding $100m of revenue to the business and could drive a further 10% uplift, worth approximately $200m revenue

You also want to determine the impact of your "so whats" on both the hypothesis—do they confirm, disprove or lead to its revision—and if it is revised, what further and new evidence you need to gather to test your revised hypothesis.

Use the following questions to refine your insights into "so whats" and to determine the impact on your hypotheses and on further evidence required:

1. **What is the evidence really telling me** and what is the most I can infer, both standalone and when I combine with other pieces of evidence?
2. **Is each insight really saying something meaningful** in the form of a "so what" or is it more likely to only elicit a disinterested "uh-huh?"
3. **What impact does each "so what" have on the hypotheses?**
   - Do any "so whats" confirm a hypothesis?
   - Do any "so whats" disprove a hypothesis?
   - Do any "so whats" lead to revision of a hypothesis?
   - Is the impact of any "so what" on the hypotheses significant enough for you to need to make stakeholders aware prior to next steering committee?
4. **What impact do the "so whats" have on further evidence required and/or the direction of evidence gathering?**
   - Is there any evidence you were looking to gather that you no longer need?
   - Is there new evidence required and where can you find it?

EXERCISE: THE "SO WHAT" GAME

If you are stuck and feel like your "so what" isn't saying enough then read out your "so what" to a colleague and get them to repeatedly ask you "so what", each time refining the "so what" like peeling an onion. Here's how it might go:

You: Basically, I'm just saying that customer service is important to our customers.

Friend: So what?

You: Well, it's important because it has a bearing on how easy it is to work with us and how much they want to do. Often customers contact our customer services department when they are new to us and these first experiences can determine if we become good business partners or if the relationship dwindles before it has even started.

Friend: So what?

You: Oh well, it's important as I said. But in fact our customer service is pretty good and on average as good as our competitors'.

Friend: So what?

You: It means that we should always monitor our customer services to ensure it is good enough and that there is nothing we need to do right now, no further investment required, our current service is good enough.

DOCUMENTING YOUR FINDINGS

You want to meticulously document your findings and the resulting revisions to each hypothesis, so you can show both evolution of your hypothesis and the evidence to support each evolution.

To document this information you can use D_3evelop Findings Tables, each of which comprise rows for the hypothesis and its revisions plus two columns: one for the evidence required and one for findings and implications. Since there will likely be multiple revisions of each hypothesis, it works best to have one table dedicated to each of your initial hypotheses. For ITC, this means there would be seven D_3evelop Findings Tables. Below we provide an example initial D_3evelop Findings Table for hypothesis A, Building overseas sales teams, labeled v.1 of the table.

D_3EVELOP EVIDENCE TABLE, HYPOTHESIS A, V.1	
ORIGINAL HYPOTHESIS	
A. Overseas sales teams	
Grow profit in Canada, UK and Germany by 50% by marketing overseas capabilities to US customers	
(estimated profit per year = profit outside US x 50% = 15% x $35m x 50% = $2.6m, less costs to be calculated)	
Evidence Required	**Findings & Implications**

• Understand from existing US customers:
  - Their satisfaction
  - Their needs outside US
  - How those needs are serviced today
  - Interest in ITC providing those services	

Just as your hypothesis will evolve in this "washing machine phase", so will your D_3evelop Findings Tables.

In its first form, as in v.1 for hypothesis A above, your D_3evelop Findings Table will list your initial hypothesis and the required evidence and the findings and implications column will be empty, as per the example above.

Every time you have new findings, consider their implications on your hypothesis and whether they lead to its confirmation, rejection or revision. Ultimately you'll need to either prove or disprove your hypothesis but it's likely that it will be revised and then tested several times in this "washing machine phase" before it can be confirmed or rejected.

Each time your findings lead you to revise your hypothesis, add a new row to your table. In this new row, list the revised hypothesis and in the rows below add the evidence required. Initially the findings and implications column will be blank, as per the example below v.2, since you've not gathered and reviewed your evidence yet.

D₃EVELOP EVIDENCE TABLE, HYPOTHESIS A, V.2

ORIGINAL HYPOTHESIS

A. Overseas sales teams

Grow profit in Canada, UK and Germany by 50% by marketing overseas capabilities to US customers

(estimated profit per year = profit outside US x 50% = 15% x $35m x 50% = $2.6m, less costs to be calculated)

Evidence Required	Findings & Implications

• Understand from existing US customers:
  – Their satisfaction
  – Their needs outside US
  – How those needs are serviced today
  – Interest in ITC providing those services
	• Three interviews with existing customers
	• Two seriously interested in an ITC offer in Canada, UK and/or Germany
	  – [Interviews with Bellview, Infinitum and Generation X]
	• ITC already has some operations in all three countires
	  – [Confirmed by legal team]
	Implies:
	• Need for ITC's services overseas
	• No legal impediment to building business

D₃EVELOP EVIDENCE TABLE, HYPOTHESIS A, V.2
REVISED HYPOTHESIS

A. Overseas sales teams

Set up sales teams in Canada, Germany and the UK and target existing customers with operations there to at least double profitability in all three by end 2018

Estimated additional $0.9m profit per year by 2018 for each of the three markets. Total = $2.7m

Evidence Required	Findings & Implications
• Test interest with two multinational customers • Model potential profitability based on interview feedback	

Once you have gathered and reviewed your required evidence for the revised hypothesis in the new row, you can fill in the findings and implications column repeating the cycle to see if that leads to your hypothesis being confirmed, rejected or revised. You can see this next iteration in the example overleaf where the hypothesis is revised again based on the new findings and implications:

D₃EVELOP EVIDENCE TABLE, HYPOTHESIS A, V.3

ORIGINAL HYPOTHESIS

A. Overseas sales teams

Grow profit in Canada, UK and Germany by 50% by marketing overseas capabilities to US customers

(estimated profit per year = profit outside US x 50% = 15% x $35m x 50% = $2.6m, less costs to be calculated)

Evidence Required	Findings & Implications

• Understand from existing US customers:
  – Their satisfaction
  – Their needs outside US
  – How those needs are serviced today
  – Interest in ITC providing those services
	• Three interviews with existing customers
	• Two seriously interested in an ITC offer in Canada, UK and/or Germany
	  – [Interviews with Bellview, Infinitum and Generation X]
	• ITC already has some operations in all three countires
	  – [Confirmed by legal team]
	Implies:
	• Need for ITC's services overseas
	• No legal impediment to building business

REVISED HYPOTHESIS

A. Overseas sales teams

Set up sales teams in Canada, Germany and the UK and target existing customers with operations there to at least double profitability in all three by end 2018

Estimated additional $0.9m profit per year by 2018 for each of the three markets. Total = $2.7m

D₃EVELOP EVIDENCE TABLE, HYPOTHESIS A, V.3

Evidence Required	Findings & Implications

• Test interest with two multinational customers
• Model potential profitability based on interview feedback
	• Six of eight customers interviewed expressed interest in doing business with the same products/services/terms as US
	  – [Interviews with Bellview, Infinitum, Generation X, Spotlight, Excaliber, Wainwright, Decorum and Spectrum]
	• All three markets growing at least 3% per year
	  – [Analyst reports: Gartner, UBS, Morgan Stanley]
	
	Implies:
	• Unmet need overseas from ITC's existing customers plus 3%+ market growth suggests opportunity for new customers

REVISED HYPOTHESIS

A. Overseas sales teams

Set up sales teams in Canada, Germany and the UK and target existing customers with operations there to at least double profitability in all three by end 2018

Estimated additional $1m profit per year by 2018 for each of the three markets. Total = $3m

Evidence Required	Findings & Implications
• Test numbers with finance and commercial teams	

If your findings and implications lead to your hypothesis being confirmed or rejected you can conclude this at the bottom of your table, so it's clear no further testing and revisions of your hypothesis is required. An example of hypothesis A being confirmed for ITC is below:

D$_3$EVELOP EVIDENCE TABLE, HYPOTHESIS A, V.4
ORIGINAL HYPOTHESIS
A. Overseas sales teams
Grow profit in Canada, UK and Germany by 50% by marketing overseas capabilities to US customers
(estimated profit per year = profit outside US x 50% = 15% x $35m x 50% = $2.6m, less costs to be calculated)

Evidence Required	Findings & Implications

• Understand from existing US customers:
  – Their satisfaction
  – Their needs outside US
  – How those needs are serviced today
  – Interest in ITC providing those services
	• Three interviews with existing customers
	• Two seriously interested in an ITC offer in Canada, UK and/or Germany
	  – [Interviews with Bellview, Infinitum and Generation X]
	• ITC already has some operations in all three countires
	  – [Confirmed by legal team]
	Implies:
	• Need for ITC's services overseas
	• No legal impediment to building business

D₃EVELOP EVIDENCE TABLE, HYPOTHESIS A, V.4

REVISED HYPOTHESIS

A. Overseas sales teams

Set up sales teams in Canada, Germany and the UK and target existing customers with operations there to at least double profitability in all three by end 2018

Estimated additional $0.9m profit per year by 2018 for each of the three markets. Total = $2.7m

Evidence Required	Findings & Implications

• Test interest with two multinational customers
• Model potential profitability based on interview feedback
	• Six of eight customers interviewed expressed interest in doing business with the same products/services/terms as US
	  – [Interviews with Bellview, Infinitum, Generation X, Spotlight, Excaliber, Wainwright, Decorum and Spectrum]
	• All three markets growing at least 3% per year
	  – [Analyst reports: Gartner, UBS, Morgan Stanley]
	
	Implies:
	• Unmet need overseas from ITC's existing customers plus 3%+ market growth suggests opportunity for new customers

D$_3$EVELOP EVIDENCE TABLE, HYPOTHESIS A, V.4

REVISED HYPOTHESIS

A. Overseas sales teams

Set up sales teams in Canada, Germany and the UK and target existing customers with operations there to at least double profitability in all three by end 2018

Estimated additional $1m profit per year by 2018 for each of the three markets. Total = $3m

Evidence Required	Findings & Implications
• Test numbers with finance and commercial teams	• If ITC could win just 20% of their business this would double our profitability in those countries – [Confirmed by finance team]

CONFIRMED HYPOTHESIS

Set up sales teams in Canada, Germany and the UK and target existing customers with operations there to at least double profitability in all three by end 2018

Estimated additional $0.8m profit per year by 2018 for each of the three markets. Total = $2.4m

It can take many iterations to precisely confirm or reject each hypothesis. Don't shortcut, and keep going until you have robust evidence to prove or disprove your hypotheses.

Include your D$_3$evelop Findings Tables in your *Discovery Document*. You can find further examples of D$_3$evelop Evidence Tables for other hypotheses for ITC in the *Discovery Document* at www.insightconsults.com.

CONFIRMING AND REJECTING HYPOTHESES

As your evidence builds, you want to determine when you have sufficiently proved or disproved a hypothesis. A revised hypothesis is still work-in-progress: it is in the "washing machine" and needs to keep being "washed" with evidence and revised accordingly so that it can ultimately be proved or disproved.

You need to be confident that your findings are robust and supported with evidence. In some cases, you can get evidence that immediately proves or disproves a hypothesis. For example, suppose you have a hypothesis that suggests entering a certain geographic market, then suppose that you find that this market is well-served, customers are happy, the businesses serving them are not making much money and you would need special licenses to work there that typically take two years to obtain. All this points very strongly to disproving the hypotheses about entering this market.

But often the reading of the evidence is more nuanced. For example, what if customers are not well served and the businesses operating there are making a lot of money. Notwithstanding the license issue, would it still be worth entering the market?

In such a case, it is often through getting additional evidence and then reviewing all the evidence and its implications that you then weigh the evidence overall. This can then be used to determine if a hypothesis is true, not true or partially true and needs to be revised.

You want to make sure that all your key "so whats", that is the insights from your evidence, are reflected in your final articulation of the hypotheses. Where they are of a lesser importance, include them in the supporting evidence. You also need to know when to stop gathering evidence, when what you have is good enough.

Be aware of curiosity for the sake of curiosity. Doing research and gathering new evidence is not necessarily the most effective use of time and can mean your intellect is taking over, with evidence at the expense of practical outcomes. While I am a huge fan of facts, there is undoubtedly a balance to be struck between:

- Judiciously chosen pieces of evidence, versus
- A sea of evidence that has quantity but not necessarily quality.

Two key tactics to avoid this are:

1. Keep seeking to identify the two or three pieces of information on which the hypothesis turns.
2. Remember the 80:20 rule and keep applying it to the work to be done and evidence to be gathered.

If you want to research something simply because you want to, there is nothing wrong with that. Just be clear to call it what it is and be sure not to prioritize this work above that which is absolutely required.

Taken together, the confirmed hypotheses provide the options from which you will make your choices and create your strategy.

So step back one last time, check all your D_3evelop Findings Tables and ensure that all your original hypotheses have been revised into a confirmed or rejected hypothesis,

If any hypothesis is neither proved or disproved, then stop and do the further work to test it and revise it as necessary, until it can be proved or disproved.

KEY CONCEPT: THE PARETO PRINCIPLE

The Pareto Principle, also known as the 80:20 rule, describes how often 80% of effects come from 20% of causes.

It is named after Italian economist Vilfredo Pareto, who observed in 1906 that 80% of the land in Italy was owned by 20% of the population. He further developed the principle by observing that 20% of the pea pods in his garden contained 80% of the peas.

In business this can mean:
- 80% of your revenue comes from 20% of your clients.
- 80% of your production comes from 20% of your staff.
- 80% of your sales will arise from 20% of your marketing efforts.

Applying this to evidence, it means that 20% of your evidence will provide 80% of your insights. So, consider: What are the key pieces of evidence that will yield the most important insight(s)?

Thinking 80:20 helps you avoid seeking superfluous evidence, and saves you from unnecessary use of your and your employees' time and efforts.

TRANSLATING YOUR FINDINGS INTO PROSE

Once you have your final D$_3$evelop Findings Tables you can also translate each into prose, just as we did for the pyramids related to the D$_2$iagnosis in chapter 2.1. This will prove helpful later when you come to communicate your confirmed and rejected hypotheses. Following this approach you can write the your confirmed hypothesis, with implications indented and supported evidence indented once more, as per the example below:

- Overseas sales teams: Set up sales teams in Canada, Germany and the UK and target existing customers with operations there to at least double profitability in all three by end 2018
  - Established need for ITC's services overseas plus growth overall in these markets, suggesting opportunity also for new customers.
    - Six of eight customers interviewed expressed interest in doing business with the same products/services and terms as in the US.
    - All three are growing markets in services of at least 3% per year.
    - If ITC could win just 20% of their business this would equate to a doubling of our profitability in those countries.
  - No legal impediment to building business in any of Canada, Germany and UK.
    - Already have some operations in each of the three countries.

Since this is more an output of your findings you don't need to include previous versions of the hypothesis nor any unused evidence. This was however very important to document as you were working through your hypothesis, hence the use of the D$_3$evelop Findings Table to capture it.

KEY CONCEPT: GOOD DOCUMENTATION

I think of the *Discovery Document* as my loyal friend—it stores my best thoughts and findings, remembers all the things I would otherwise forget, reminds me what further research I need to do and by reminding me constantly of the question I am seeking to answer, it makes sure I can't go too far off track. Updating the *Discovery Document* helps clarify my thinking and make sense of all the new information I am absorbing.

It also provides an excellent communication tool for the strategy design team and for updating your steering committee. During the middle weeks of the strategy design process—typically weeks six through ten of a fourteen week process—the *Discovery Document* provides the backbone for all discussions with the strategy design team and with the steering committee. It gets the important points across without requiring the strategy design leader or team to spend half the week prior to the steering committee meeting on writing a PowerPoint deck, time that would be much better spent on gathering and reviewing new information.

At times you'll have really striking insights that would come out better in the form of a chart rather than prose or bullets. In this case, there is of course nothing to stop you from creating a chart and inserting it into the *Discovery Document* alongside the relevant D_3evelop Findings Table.

The time you invest in a well-structured and maintained *Discovery Document* will pay off when you come to make choices and craft the story of these choices and of the resulting strategy.

FINALIZING YOUR LIST OF CONFIRMED HYPOTHESES

Place your final revisions of your original hypotheses into the third and last of our tables for the D$_3$evelop step: D$_3$evelop Conclusions Table, which lists all the confirmed hypotheses plus those which were rejected:

D$_3$EVELOP CONCLUSIONS TABLE	
Confirmed options	
Confirmed option	**Estimated impact**
A. Overseas sales teams: Set up sales teams in Canada, Germany and the UK and target existing customers with operations there to at least double profitability in all three by end 2018	This is estimated to yield an additional $0.8m profit in each of the three countries by 2018. Total additional profit per year by 2018 **= $2.4m**
C. Recycling: Offer cradle-to-grave recycling modularized services for all hardware including that not purchased from ITC, service includes filing of all associated paperwork	Revenue from customers 20k each with 50 customers by 2018 =$1m per year Revenue from metal traders = $0.15m recyclable material per customer x 50 customers x sold @10% = $0.75m Cost to deliver services = 6 people x$0.1m =$0.6m Total additional profit per year by 2018 = $1m +$0.75m -$0.6m **= $1.15m**

D₃EVELOP CONCLUSIONS TABLE	
Confirmed options	
Confirmed option	Estimated impact
D. New contracts: Win three new contracts of at least $75m and $2m profit per year	Assume $0.93m profit per contract per year, reduced by 30% to $0.66m per contract per year Total additional profit per year by 2018 = **$2m**
E. Webshop: By creating easy to navigate webshop, can increase small and medium business by 5% and conduct 80% of small and medium business and 40% of large business online	This will increase profits with additional revenue of $1m and cost savings of $0.3m. Total additional profit per year by 2018 = **$1.3m**
F. Modularized services: The creation of a modularized services offer, decoupling existing services packages, and with flexible à la carte choice of services	**With a webshop in place,** increase ITC's medium business by at least 20% and double small business = $4.15m profit per year less additional advertising costs of $250k = $3.9m **Without a webshop,** assume a 30% increase in small business and a 10% increase in medium business. Total additional profit per year by 2018 = **$2.1m**
Total estimated impact	**Up to a maximum of $10.8m**

D_3EVELOP CONCLUSIONS TABLE	
Rejected hypotheses	
Hypothesis	Impact
B. Cost-savings share: For managed services customers, create a cost-savings share model	N/A
G. Slow moving stock: Sell off slow moving stock more effectively to save $1m per year	N/A

CHECKING FOR SUFFICIENCY

Let's step back and determine if the options we have confirmed for ITC are sufficient to meet our goal. From our D_3evelop Conclusions Table we see that our confirmed options collectively yield up to an estimated $10.8m. Since our gap to reach our $50m profit goal is $8m, this means we are in the fortunate position of having more than sufficient options.

Your confirmed hypotheses now become your options from which to choose your strategy and you can begin the forth step D_4**ecide**

D₃EVELOP TESTING HYPOTHESES CHECKLIST

- Relevant evidence has been identified to test each hypothesis.
- You are aware of confirmation bias and have taken measures to mitigate it.
- Sources are provided for each piece of evidence.
- The range of sources is broad and often encompasses both data and interviews.
- Where assumptions have been made, these are explicit.
- Fair implications and "so whats" are drawn from the evidence.
- You have tested each of your hypotheses and through the washing machine phase, they have become confirmed or rejected.
- You have assessed the potential impact and ease of implementation of each confirmed hypothesis.

D₁efine

D₂iagnose

D₃evelop

D₄ecide

D₅eliver

4.1

MAKE CHOICES

"Life is the sum of all your choices."

Albert Camus

Strategy in 5D

Step	Chapter	Actions
D_1efine	1.1 Define Your Goal	Articulate goal as question ↓ Brainstorm sub-questions
	1.2 Map Your Domain	Structure sub-questions
D_2iagnose	2.1 Diagnose Your Situation	Gather facts ↓ Draw insights ↓ Share findings
D_3evelop	3.1 Generate Hypotheses	Develop hypotheses ↓ Gather evidence
	3.2 Test Hypotheses	Repeat until hypotheses confirmed or disproved ↓ Draw insights ↓ Share findings
D_4ecide	4.1 Make Choices	Review combinations Debate scenarios
	4.2 Write Your Strategy	Document choices
D_5eliver	5.1 Communicate Your Strategy	Communicate strategy ↓ Pilot approach
	5.2 Deliver Results	Adapt approach ↓ Track progress
ARC at every step		

KEY IDEAS

Strategy is about choices: what you choose to do—and what you choose not to do—to take you from where you are today, to where you want to get to. You have rigorously tested each of your hypotheses and have determined which of these can be confirmed as options to meet your overall goal. With a set of options available, this signals that you are ready to engage the techniques of step D_4 and put together your strategy: it's time to D_4ecide.

Start by assessing each option. To determine this we use the **FLIRT** acronym, the first four letters cover assessing the Financial impact (**F**), Limitations/dependencies (**L**), ease of Implementation (**I**), level of Risk (**R**) for each option individually.

An evaluation of each option is however insufficient when choosing a combination of options. Thought must also be given to potential synergies or conflicts between options as most importantly, you need a combination of options that work well together (**T**), which completes FLIRT.

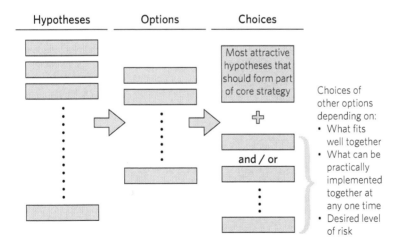

Hypotheses	Options	Choices

Most attractive hypotheses that should form part of core strategy

and / or

Choices of other options depending on:
• What fits well together
• What can be practically implemented together at any one time
• Desired level of risk

Figure 31: From hypotheses to choices

The best choices come from reviewing different combinations of options, what these could deliver, and collectively, how difficult these will be to deliver. This means that you will not necessarily be choosing the top three options based on their individual assessment. For example, suppose you have six options and that option one could not be implemented alongside either option two or three (and vice versa). Then your feasible combinations of options are likely to be either combining option one with options four onwards, or combining options two and three, with options four onwards, and it is one of these combinations of options that should form your strategy.

Remember, strategy is about choices, and is as much about what you choose not to do, as what you choose to do. You need to be realistic about how much your organization can do at any one time. Choosing not to do something now does not mean you will never do it. Yet avoiding making a choice is also a choice. So be as explicit about what you will not do as what you will do. Also think about what you will prioritize to go first and why, since cleverly and realistically sequencing your choices makes all the difference to your chances of success. Better to be realistic and put some options on hold, with the opportunity to return to them in a year or two, once you have successfully delivered other choices.

Be sure to schedule sufficient discussion time with the strategy design team and with wider stakeholders. Given you have done all this hard work to generate and test your hypotheses, you want time to debate your choices, ensuring that they draw solely on the confirmed options and that they are rigorously and objectively assessed using **FLIRT**.

And yes, you guessed it, it's all recorded in your *Discovery Document*, making it easy to understand the rationale for choices in the future. If you provide transparency, documenting the evidence and assessments for all of your choices, then when a change in the external environment occurs—which inevitably will happen at some point—you will have a rich set of information at your fingertips that enabling you to quickly determine the implication(s) of the change and whether this then affects your choices and your strategy.

Schedule sufficient time to craft your communication of these choices. You want to communicate your choices clearly and logically, showing how you reached your recommendation set of choices

An excellent way to communicate your strategy is to structure your thinking using the Minto Pyramid Principle® which was introduced in chapter 2.1 and which groups and links information logically, providing a structured way to draw out implications.

The great news is that you have already done most of the work to structure communication of your choices. What remains is to finalize any documentation of evidence and reasoning for proposed choices and ensure this all flows as a story. Then to ensure appropriate context, recap the work you did to get here including providing the context to your original question, a synthesis of your diagnosis and listing the hypotheses you tested.

Once you have your story, if you choose to communicate it using slides, you want to create a storyboard. This is a translation of your storyline into a set of slide titles that in succession tell your story. You can check this by reading your slide titles out loud in order, adding no further words. If your titles alone convey all key parts of your story, you have succeeded.

Then, just as you did before when you created your initial dummy deck containing the diagnosis and hypotheses slides, you include on each slide an outline of the evidence to be included that will support the "so what" in the slide title. Following the design and formatting guidelines in chapter 2.1, you can create a full presentation recapping your diagnosis and recommending a combination of choices that will form your strategy.

DELIVERABLES, CONCEPTS, ARC AND MEETINGS

Step	Chapter	Key Concepts	Deliverables
D$_4$ecide	4.1 Make Choices	FLIRT (Financial, Limitations, Implementation, Risk Together)	D$_4$ecide Table D$_4$ecide Document
		Storyline	
		Storyboard	
		ORCAS	
		TOADS	

Examples of applying ARC when making choices are:

- The combination of choices are **actionable** and are realistically sequenced.
- Time is put aside to **rigorously** discuss different combinations of options.
- The approach is **collaborative**, facilitating buy-in and granting everyone the opportunity to assess which options they would choose and why.

The key meetings required to complete this chapter are:

- Strategy design team:
  - First meeting to review combinations of options to meet goal and to discuss assessment of individual options and their combinations according to FLIRT. Also identify gaps or disagreements in the assessment and any information required to complete the assessment.
  - Second meeting: debate final assessment of combinations of options and what this yields as the recommended combination of options.
  - Third meeting (and further meetings as needed) to review the story and storyboard including reading the slide titles of the storyboard out loud multiple times to refine them until they fully and accurately tell the story,

- Steering committee:
  - First meeting to review FLIRT assessment of combinations of options and to identify any gaps or disagreements in the assessment.
  - Second meeting to review recommended combination of choices and come to final alignment on these choices.

SUFFICIENCY, FLIRT AND THE D$_4$ECIDE TABLE

Just as in the previous steps D$_2$iagnose and D$_3$evelop, we begin with sub-questions related to this step. We again use a table—the D$_4$ecide Table—once more putting the most detailed tier of sub-questions related to this step into the first column. In the top half of the table, the other columns contain each possible option individually. In the lower half of the table, the columns contain each of the possible combinations of options which could meet our goal:

D$_4$ECIDE TABLE					
	Possible options				
Sub-questions	**A**	**C**	**D**	**E**	**F**
6.1 What is the financial potential of each option?	Assess per option				
6.2 What are the limitations, what is each option dependent on?	Assess per option				
6.3 How easy is it to implement each option?	Assess per option				
6.4 What is the level of risk for each option, and how can this be mitigated?	Assess per option				

D$_4$ECIDE TABLE	
	Possible combinations
6.5 What combinations of options are sufficient to meet your goal, and how does each combination fare when assessed in the same way as each option?	Add in one combination per column, adding more columns if necessary
	Assess each combination

ITC's D$_4$eliver sub-questions, as listed in the D$_4$eliver Table, should not be thought of as specific to ITC. They reflect the questions you need to ask when weighing up different options, almost regardless of topic. Given the more universal nature of these sub-questions, I like to use the acronym **FLIRT**, which captures the key criteria you need to consider and makes it much more catchy than a list of questions:

Financial The expected financial impact plus any one-off setup costs. Impact is most commonly assessed over a three year period.

Limitations Anything on which this is dependent on to succeed.

Implementation What it will take to implement and the ease of doing it. Often assessed as Low/Medium/High.

Risk The risks and the what extent to which these be mitigated. Often assessed as Low/Medium/High.

Together The possible combinations of options, how these stack up when assessed against the first four criteria—F, L, I and R—and how the combination be sequenced.

For ITC, each letter of the acronym correlates to the sub-questions 6.1 through 6.5 in turn. This may be similar, or you might find one letter of the FLIRT acronym relates to more than one sub-questions. In either case, this enables us to rewrite our D_4ecide Table as follows:

D₄ECIDE TABLE					
	Possible options				
Sub-questions	A	C	D	E	F
Financial	Assess per option				
L imitations	Assess per option				
I mplementation	Assess per option				
R isk	Assess per option				
	Possible combinations				
T ogether	Add in one combination per column, adding more columns if necessary				
	Assess each combination				

WEIGHING UP COMBINATIONS OF OPTIONS

Now you have your D$_4$ecide Table, there is one final step before commencing the assessment of options and combinations: determining all the possible combinations that could deliver your goal, which you then put in separate columns in the lower part of the table.

We want to determine these possible combinations for ITC, but first let's think about the principles behind weighing up different combinations.

Suppose you have three confirmed options in three distinct markets, with the following characteristics:

Market 1: Reasonable demand for your existing products and services. Sales and marketing today has poor reach to this market.

Market 2: Strong demand. Needs are complex and not met by today's products and services. Would likely to need to quickly and continually innovate your products and services to keep these customers.

Market 3: Highest demand and projected growth rate. However, 50% risk of new regulations that could severely affect your ability to serve this market competitively.

These are all legitimate options—but that does not mean that these become your strategy. These options are the set of possible strategic choices about where to play and what to offer. Choosing one option could rule out another, or rule in another if there are dependencies.

You have a goal to deliver, and yet you also need to be realistic as to how many options you could deliver at any one time. It may be that your options are compatible from a dependency perspective but that is not realistic to them implement together. To some extent, this depends on your organization's size and bandwidth. If, for example, you are a small organization, it may be that your best chance of success would be to focus first on one option and get it working before starting on another. Yet even if you are a large corporation, taking on lots of initiatives simultaneously rarely works. Better for a few options to succeed and to grow from there.

The order in which you make your choices also plays a role, since your first choice determines what else you can and should do—the second choice further defines what else you can and should do—and so on until your choices are exhausted. This means it makes sense to play out different combinations of options which begin with different "first choices".

It is worth noting that often there is convergence on one or two options that everyone agrees should be part of the strategy and so be sure that each of these are considered as a "first choice" when you play out the different combinations.

In our example here, with three different markets, you could choose to start in Market 1 with the least growth potential but where products and services are the best match, and build up sales and marketing capability. Or you could decide to start with Market 3 and make the most of the highest growth in the short term, knowing the opportunity may then disappear. In that instance, you want to have another option to work on in the background which could compensate for the profit that might be lost in Market 3 if the new regulations do come into force.

Some years ago, I was asked to lead a division whose strategy I had written (prior to working in the division). So much for the theoretical calculations I had previously shared from the outside on how much gross margin percentage could be improved, now I had to do it. This only has to happen to you once before you truly understand the difference between a plan that sounds marvelous in principle and one that can actually be delivered. Think about it—if you were fully responsible for delivery of the strategy, could you make it work? Step back and remind yourself of the original question and reflect on the combination of options that will best fulfill this goal for your organization, and can be delivered—and then choose.

DETERMINING VIABLE COMBINATIONS OF OPTIONS

Let's return to our D_4ecide Table to which we need to add all possible combinations of options in the columns in the lower part of the table.

From the D_3evelop Conclusions Table at the end of the last chapter, we already know the possible options from which we can create combinations of options, and as a recap, we provide a summary version of this table below.

Since there are different estimates for modularized services depending on whether the webshop is built or not, we include both and use F and F_E to denote the two options, where F_E denotes the implementation of both F and E.

Here is a summary version of the D_3evelop Conclusions Table:

D_3EVELOP CONCLUSIONS TABLE (SUMMARY)	
Option	Estimated impact (additional annual profit by 2018)
A. Overseas sales teams	$2.4m
C. Recycling	$1.15m
D. New contracts	$2.0m
E. Webshop	$1.3m
F. Modularized services	F_E = $3.9m F = $2.1m
Total estimated impact	Up to a maximum of $10.8m

Our goal is to deliver $50m profit by 2018, and we have a $8m shortfall. From the D_4evelop Conclusions Table, we can see that our options collectively yield $10.8m, which is sufficient to meet our goal.

Our question therefore becomes: which combinations of these options can deliver at least $8m additional profit by 2018?

Let's start by considering the option with the highest financial impact, F_E, as our "first choice" If we choose this option, then by definition we need E too, which together yield \$5.2m (= \$3.9m + \$1.3m).

From here, to bridge the \$8m gap, we need an additional \$2.8m (= \$8m - \$5.2m), so alone each of A, D and C are insufficient.

If we take A as our next and third choice after F_E and E, then adding either C or D is sufficient:

F_E, E, A, C = \$8.8m

F_E, E, A, D = \$9.6m

If we instead take C as our next and third choice, then adding A or D is sufficient, and since we already have a combination with A and C (the impact of the combination is the same even if the options are in a different order) then we just add the combination with C and D:

F_E, E, D, C = \$8.4m

If we take D as our third choice, then adding either C or A is sufficient and we have both those combinations included above.

Now let's consider F as our "first choice". By definition, there is no E, then even adding all other options A, C and D we have

F, A, C, D = \$7.7m, which is insufficient.

With no F nor F_E at all and any of A, C, D E as "first choice" and adding in all other options we have:

A, C, D, E= \$ 6.9m,

which is insufficient

So there are three combinations of options from which to choose.
   i. F_E, E, A, D = \$9.6m
   ii. F_E, E, A, C = \$8.8m
   iii. F_E, E, D, C = \$8.4m

Returning to our D_4ecide Table, this means that we have three columns in the lower part of the table overleaf:

D$_4$ECIDE TABLE					
	Possible Options				
Sub-questions	A	C	D	E	F$_E$
Financial	Assess per option				
L imitations	Assess per option				
I mplementation	Assess per option				
Risk	Assess per option				
	Possible Combinations				
Together	F$_E$, E, A, D		F$_E$, E, A, C		F$_E$, E, D, C
	Assess each combination				

ASSESSING YOUR OPTIONS

Now we have all the parameters for our D$_4$ecide Table in place, including the three possible combinations of options, it works well to begin an assessment of each option using the first part of the FLIRT criteria.

Take all the options featuring in your combinations – for ITC this is A, C, D, E, F$_E$, - and apply the first four parts of FLIRT. Think through and then document your assumptions and assessment of each option in the D$_4$ecide Table.

You are likely to be able to fill in some parts of the assessment straightaway—for example you will already have estimated the financial impact but you may require more thinking and work to determine one-off costs, to get clear on any limitations and to assess risk.

While the assessment needs to be rigorous and fact-based, inevitably since it is an assessment of what will happen in the future, there may be different assessments of the same information. For example, you may agree on the risks of one particular option but one person may be more optimistic than another on the ability to mitigate it.

Given the nature of the assessment it makes sense for the strategy design team to work together on it and to come to alignment on the assessment of each option.

If you are struggling to align on the assessment of certain options, come to alignment on what further evidence will be gathered and reviewed to enable a second discussion.

Depending on the involvement of your steering committee and if any of the assessments are surprising, you may also want to discuss with them, rather than wait to discuss alongside the different possible combinations of options.

Overleaf is a completed upper part of the D_4ecide Table for ITC:

D_4ECIDE TABLE, UPPER PART			
Option(s)	**A. Overseas sales teams**	**C. Recycling**	
Financial (annual net impact in 3 years' time plus one-off costs)	$2.4m One-off costs assumed in ongoing profit	$1.2m One-off cost to build services $0.25m	
L imitations (specify what)	None	None	
I mplementation (ease of implementation L|M|H)	Medium Requires recruiting new sales staff in each of Canada, Germany and the UK, where already have operations	Low/Medium Have thorough understanding of regulation; some design work to determine full set of services	
Risk (L|M|H have included ability to mitigate)	Low Financial cost of new team members ($1.7m rising to $3.4m) Small reputational risk	Medium Commodity prices and recycling values can dramatically swing profitability	
Together (sequencing)	n/a	n/a	

D. New contracts	E. Webshop	F. Modularized services
$2.0 No one-off costs	$1.3m One-off build cost of $2m	F_E: $3.9m or F: $2.1m One-off costs, training of $20k then $10k first two years Ongoing costs of advertising included in above expected impact
None	None	Dependency E. Webshop required for larger impact
High Good new business track record Team already in place with capabilities to deliver this	Low/Medium Requires significant technology build	Medium Requires marketing effort to modularize existing packaged services; limited redesign required
Low/Medium This type of initiative sounds obvious but will not work unless something different is in place (else it would have already happened)	Medium Test all key elements of webshop with customers before full launch to ensure will give what they need	Medium Lots of piloting of proposed services with existing clients mitigates risk of poor design
n/a	Important Needs to commence straightaway to support F_E	n/a

You can plot the aspects F and I on a prioritization matrix. You could also plot L and R on another 2x2 matrix.

Prioritization Matrix

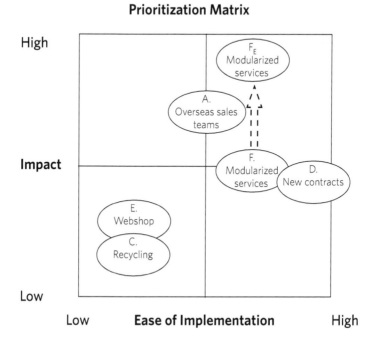

Figure 32: Confirmed options plotted on prioritization matrix

ASSESSING YOUR COMBINATIONS

Now repeat FLIRT for the different combinations of options.

The assessment of the combination of options is not just the sum of the individual assessments. For example, two medium risk options can together become much more risky or can mitigate the each other's risk, reducing the overall risk. Only an analysis of the combination can tell you that; a summing of the assessments of each individual option in the combinations would miss this. Hence starting with an individual assessment of each option and then being able to step back and review the combination set a unit.

For ITC, since all three combinations of options have two of the four options in common—F_E and E—then the heart of what we are weighing up is which two of A: Overseas sales teams, D: New contracts or C: Recycling are easiest to do and which most limit risk, where risk includes the least strategic risk and most balanced combination of options to the organization.

Option D: New contracts, is easiest to implement and does not pull on already used resources . From a risk perspective, if we don't choose A: Overseas sales teams, then we reinforce ITC's dependence on US business. If we choose C: Recycling, we also choose a second new services option alongside F_E and this will draw on the same resources.

You can record your assessment in the D$_4$ecide Table:

D$_4$ECIDE TABLE, LOWER PART			
Options	F_E, E, A, D	F_E, E, A, C	F_E, E, D, C
Financial	$9.6m	$8.8m	$8.4m
Limitations	None (E part of combination)	None	None
Implementation	M+	L to M	M to H
Risk	L/M Can do A in parallel without diverting service design resources for F_E	M F_E and C draw on same service design resources	M/H Continued dependence on US
Together	Begin E at once, F_E as new team and D as continuation of existing work Start recruiting for A to start in 6 months	Would not start C until year 2 to allow F_E service design work to take place	Would not start C until year 2 to allow F_E service design work to take place

FINALIZING YOUR CHOICES

Once you have a FLIRT assessment of each of the combinations, it is important to have time to review and debate each assessment as a strategy design team and then with your steering committee.

In instances where there are several possible combinations of options and quite different assessments of these, one approach is to map out different scenarios. For example, if you pursued options F_E, E, A, and D, what would that deliver?

Instead of one figure for financial impact, you can express it as a range, such as, if F_E, E, A and D perform really well then we'll deliver X and if they perform less well then we'll deliver Y. Similarly note the range of risks and views on how easy these would be to mitigate.

Then answer the same questions for options F_E, E, A and C. You can try all combinations this way and as a team work through what each combination would likely deliver.

At this point, often the optimal combination of options to pursue becomes self-evident. If that's not the case, revert back to the evidence and consider what further evidence you need to make a decision.

The D_4ecide Table for ITC indicates that the first combination F_E, E, A, D would deliver most impact and be a little easier to do than the second combination F_E, E, A, C. The third combination F_E, E, D, C is the easiest to deliver, but delivers the least.

Looking at these two sets, the first combination is less risky and comes out strongest on the FLIRT assessment – and is our choice.

You can highlight the column with your recommended combination of options in your D_4ecide Table. Be sure to list the details of how you got to your combination of options, including documenting any alternative scenarios you mapped out. That way, if questions are asked later about why certain decisions were made, you can easily provide background and evidence for these.

Like you did for the individual options, you can plot the financial impact versus ease of implementation for each combination of options, as per the matrix below:

Prioritization Matrix

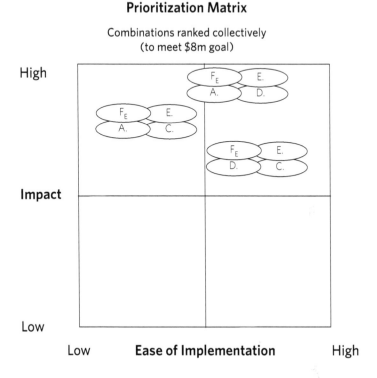

Figure 33: Prioritization matrix for combinations taken collectively

COMMUNICATION OF YOUR CHOICES: THE STORYLINE

With a combination of options in mind—your recommended choices—you now need to review these choices with your steering committee and reach alignment on them.

A great way to do this is to organize your thinking into a storyline which describes the rationale for the combination of options you are recommending and which uses the Minto Pyramid Principle® to structure your thinking. This storyline written in the form of an outline or set of bullets in prose that can then be translated into slides or a full prose document.

The great news is that you have done most of the work for your storyline already by structuring your thinking at every step of Strategy in 5D from defining the question, to conducting the diagnosis, to choosing options.

The meat of your storyline needs to be your recommended combination of options and you want to spend the majority of your time making sure you get the logic and wording for this right. But it would be a mistake to not first summarize all the other work that got you there. This is critical for two reasons: firstly, many people you share your recommendations with simply won't remember the question you started with, nor the diagnosis findings, nor the hypotheses tested. Secondly, you need to level-set so that your audience is operating from the same set of information. Otherwise you risk audience members carrying all sorts of different assumptions about the work done or using precious time in the meeting to ask questions that have already been covered.

You can use the Strategy in 5D framework to determine what you need to cover. For example, from where we are now—at the beginning of step D_4ecide—you can provide a recap of findings of the three previous steps to set up discussion of your recommended options:

- D_1efine: recap context and question.
- D_2iagnose: recap key diagnostic findings.
- D_3evelop: list hypotheses tested and which were confirmed.

Once you have established the above—ideally using no more than a few sentences in your storyline, translated to one, or at most two slides per step—then you can move into more detail on each of the confirmed hypotheses.

Later in the process, when you are in the D_5eliver step and are ready to communicate your delivery plan, continue to share three to six slides at the beginning of your document that recap key points for the D_1efine, D_2iagnose and D_3evelop steps, plus include slide(s) describing the list of choices made as part of step D_4ecide. You can often use the same initial three to six slides throughout the strategy design phase. This may sound unoriginal, but they provide a visual anchor for the audience, reminding them what topic you are there to discuss. You can often pass over the slides very quickly—sometimes I acknowledge that the slides are familiar and rather than describing them in turn, pause briefly to look at everyone to check they agree they are familiar, and then move on.

To structure the communication of your findings for the D_4**ecide** step, I suggest providing the following, which I use the acronym (and image of) ORCAS:

Options a full list of confirmed and rejected hypotheses.

Relevant evidence for each hypothesis whether confirmed or rejected.

Combinations of options, listed with all possibilities to meet the goal.

Assessment of the way each combination works together or not.

Suggested combination of options to deliver the goal.

At the risk of stating the obvious, your storyline relating to each of the steps must be grounded in what you have found. Occasionally on my strategy courses I see people at this stage write a storyline totally divorced from all their findings. You want to do quite the reverse—your storyline is a pithy synthesis of all your key findings.

EXAMPLE STORYLINE

The following is an example storyline for ITC. While there is quite a bit of information to include, you want the key points of your story to be really clear, such that a child could follow:

Step D$_1$efine (recap):

[The following is taken directly from the D$_1$efine Question Frame in chapter 1.1, page 42].

- Over the past three years, ITC has experienced 8% revenue growth, yielding $360m in 2015. Profitability has been flat in this same period and in 2015 was $38m.
- A corporate plan estimated $42m profit for 2018, but this was rejected by the leadership team as insufficiently ambitious.
- The CEO believes the next two years are critical to reinvigorating the company and kick-starting a growth trajectory and this requires reaching $50m profit.
- Question being addressed is: what actions can ITC best take to develop capabilities and achieve sustainable profit of at least $50m per year from 2018?

Step D$_2$iagnosis (recap):

[The following is taken directly from chapter 2.1, from page 135].

To meet $50m profit goal by 2018, ITC will need generate $8m beyond plan:

- Strategy in need of revision to encompass plans in services.
- Current projections fall short of three year profit target by $8m.
- Heavy reliance on USA for revenue and profit.
- Reliance on 17 customers with more than half of this revenue up for tender next three years.
- Competitor success coming from focus on specific customer groups with targeted offerings.
- Opportunity to create modularized services offer, particularly for medium and small businesses and to explore offering a cost-savings share model.
- Opportunity to extend existing end-of-life recycling offer.

Step D₃evelop (recap):

[The following is taken directly from directly from the D₃evelop Evidence Table in chapter 3.1, page 159].

The list of hypotheses we tested:
- **Overseas sales teams:** By better marketing international capabilities to existing multinational customers in the US, can increase overall business by 50% in each of Canada, UK and continental Europe (estimate $2.6m profit).
- **Cost-savings share:** For managed services customers, create a cost-savings share model (estimate $0.5m profit per year based on $100k profit per customer and five customers).
- **Recycling:** Extend existing end-of-life recycling offer to add 3% to revenue and profit (estimate $1m additional profit based on average add to each customer).
- **New contracts:** Win three new contracts in next three years of at least $100m and min $3m profit per year ($1m each).
- **Modularized services:** The creation of a modularized services offer, with flexible à la carte choice of services could increase US market share by 1% in each of small and medium business markets (estimate $3.25m additional profit).
- **Webshop:** By creating a robust webshop, can conduct 50% of product business online, saving $1m per year (after upfront investment costs to build, estimate $2m).
- **Slow-moving stock:** Sell off slow moving stock more effectively to save an estimated $1m per year.

Step D₄ecide (full commentary):

[Recommended options structured into five areas outlined on page 229, using the acronym ORCAS as an aide-memoire.]

1. **Options:** Seven options reviewed of which five confirmed and two rejected [from D₃evelop Conclusions Table, chapter 3.2, from page 200].
   - Overseas sales teams, modularized services, webshop, new contracts, and recycling were confirmed as options.
   - Cost-savings share and slow-moving stock were rejected.

2. **Relevant evidence:** Option A, Overseas sales teams: Set up sales teams in Canada, Germany and the UK and target existing customers with operations there to at least double profitability in all three by end 2018. [Confirmed hypothesis from D_3evelop Evidence Table, chapter 3.2, from page 190. Evidence and findings below taken from same table.]
   - Unmet need for ITC's services overseas from existing customers plus 3%+ growth suggests opportunity also for new customers.
     - Six of eight customers interviewed expressed interest in doing business with the same products/services and terms as in the US.
     - If ITC could win 20% of their business this would double our profitability in those countries.
   - No legal impediment to building business in any of Canada, Germany and UK where already have businesses.
     - Already have operations in each of the three countries.
     - Estimate additional $0.8m per country profit.

...and so on for the remaining four confirmed hypotheses and for the two rejected hypotheses.

3. **Combinations of options:** There are three combinations of options to meet the $8m goal. [Add from D_4ecide Table from this chapter, see page 220].
   - i: F_E, E, A, D,
   - ii: F_E, E, A, C,
   - iii: F_E, E, D, C
4. **Assessment of combinations:** Impact for each of the five confirmed hypotheses ranges from $1.2m to $3.9m, with a range of low, medium and high ease of implementation. The assessment of the three possible combinations highlights differing impact, ease of implementation and risk [Can add full D_4ecide Table from page 225 here.]
5. **Recommended combination of options:** Based on FLIRT assessment, recommended combination of choices are F_E, E, A, D: modularized services, webshop, new contracts and overseas sales teams to yield $9.6m.

Once you have your draft storyline in place, make sure that you are sharing evidence to substantiate all you are saying. No more evidence than necessary of course, but no less either—don't let all your work gathering evidence go to waste. You want to also ensure that you include sources for your evidence—both to add credibility and as a guide to someone who may read this much later.

Then step back and reread the overall question. Ask yourself whether your storyline addresses the overall question and if there is anything still missing.

KEY CONCEPT: GOOD STORYLINE PRACTICE

- A great storyline articulates your key thoughts clearly, logically and with fluidity. Check that your storyline:
- Is a direct and accurate translation of your findings and "so whats" into a story.
- Uses the Minto Pyramid Principle® as a way to structure findings and implications.
- Expresses your key findings and "so whats". No "so whats" are missing and no new "so whats" or findings suddenly appear for the first time or are cited without evidence.
- Provides sufficient but not superfluous evidence.
- Tells a story that moves towards solutions to the overall question.

FROM STORYLINE TO STORYBOARD

The storyboard is the translation of your storyline into slides. Just as you did for your dummy deck, you create your storyboard by taking a piece of paper and manually dividing it up into boxes to represent your slides. This allows you to see all slides at once in one place. Since the slides are in sequence, once you add your slide titles—from the key points of your storyline—you can visualize the flow of the full presentation.

As I mentioned in chapter 2.1, I prefer to use paper. If you use PowerPoint, be sure to resist starting to work on the details on each slide, or you will lose the overall sense of flow, to the great detriment of the story you need to communicate.

Since you will inevitably change the title order and wording several times, I use a pencil and eraser and have a few pieces of paper on hand if I need to redraw or add more slides. I then follow the following five actions, using another animal acronym to help me remember—**TOADS**:

Titles: Write, the key points of your storyline, in order, as the titles of your slides. If you have spent time to make your storyline flow with pithy "so whats", then this exercise is very fast, you are simply translating the key points into slide titles.

Out loud: Now read the slide titles out loud. Don't just contemplate it, do it. This may sound strange, but it doesn't work the same if you do it in your head.

Assign: Transfer supporting evidence for each slide title onto each slide. At this stage it is sufficient to write the evidence in text plus how you might present it rather than write it out in full.

Design: Sketch out the best design for each slide to present the supporting evidence.

Sources: Add to each slide, referencing all evidence.

Reading out loud without adding anything superfluous quickly identifies any gaps allowing you to amend your slide titles, and add or remove slides as required. Don't move on until you are happy that your slide titles work precisely as articulated.

It is worth noting that between the **Out loud** and **Assign** steps of TOADS, there is a crucial check-in phase. Having read your titles aloud, first feel if you have conveyed all of your key messages. If there is anything missing, add it; anything superfluous, remove it.

Ask yourself: do the titles flow? Are they in the right order? Play around with the order of slides until it really flows.

Also do a quick practical check that you do not have too many slides for your meeting. A good rule of thumb is two minutes per slide. You can put additional slides into an appendix and refer to them if detailed questions come up.

In the strategy courses I run, one of the coaching sessions begins with me asking you to come with your storyboard and for you to present to me, only articulating the titles of each slide, with no attention paid to any content that will go on the slides. Often I ask people to read the titles to me in succession two or three times. This is very insightful as you very quickly feel whether your slide titles capture all you want to say, and whether they flow. Thanks to this exercise, people regularly make small and sometimes big changes to clarify specific titles or to add or remove titles or slides, as well as changes to the order of the titles or slides, to make them flow more easily.

On the following pages is an example storyboard for ITC based on the storyline with the first three parts of the acronym—Title, Out loud, Assign—complete and with more work to be done to complete Design and Sources.

If you compare these with the storyline above you will notice some small differences where slide titles or content have been refined for the logic and flow to work.

Goal set for $50m profit in 2018, up from $38m in 2015

- Over the past three years, ITC has experienced 8% revenue growth, yielding $360m in 2015. Profitability has been flat in this same period and in 2015 was $38m
- A corporate plan estimated $42m profit for 2018, but this was rejected by the leadership team as insufficiently ambitious
- The CEO believes the next two years are critical to reinvigorating the company and kick-starting a growth trajectory and require reaching $50m profit

To meet $50m profit goal by 2018, ITC will need to generate $8m beyond plan

- Strategy in need of revision to encompass plans in services
- Current projections fall short of three year profit target by $8m
- Heavy reliance on USA for revenue and profit
- Dependence on 17 customers with more than half of this revenue up for tender in the next three years
- Competitor success coming from focus on specific customer groups with targeted offerings
- Opportunity to create modularized services offer, particularly for medium and small businesses and to explore offering a cost-savings share model

> RIGHT NOW THIS SLIDE IS A DATA DUMP. NEED TO PRESENT INFORMATION VISUALLY IN ONE OR MORE SLIDES

Seven opportunities reviewed of which five confirmed and two rejected

Confirmed hypotheses	Rejected hypotheses
• Modularized services	• Cost savings share model
• Overseas sales team	• Slow-moving stock
• New contracts	
• Webshop	
• Recycling	

Modularized services could yield $3.9m incremental profit per year provided webshop also implemented

- Nearly all smaller customers interviewed talked about the need for more flexibility to buy only the services they need. Packaged offerings restricts them from buying from ITC
- Technology Partners has experienced significant growth following the route of modularized services and webshop
- No new services design needed to modularize services—this is about marketing and pricing appropriately
- No additional cost beyond advertising/promotions budget—design can be done by in-house marketing team—estimated at $250k per year
- With webshop in place, it's possible to double the number of small businesses and increase medium size by 20%. This would generate $4.15m profit per year less additional advertising costs of $250k, yielding $3.9m per year additional profits
- Without a webshop, can increase small business by 30% and medium business by 10%, this would generate $2.1m per year additional profits

> RIGHT NOW THIS SLIDE IS A DATA DUMP. NEED TO
> PRESENT INFORMATION VISUALLY IN ONE OR MORE SLIDES

Overseas sales teams in Canada, Germany and the UK and target existing customers with operations in these three countries

- Established need for our services overseas with customers who trust us plus growth overall in these markets, suggesting opportunity also for new customers
- Of eight interviews with existing customers with operations in at least one of Canada, Germany and the UK, five said they would be seriously interested in doing business with us there, with the same products/services and terms as in the US
- All three are growing markets in services of at least 3% per year
- If we could win just 20% of their business this would equate to a doubling of our profitability in those countries
- No legal impediment to building business in either Canada, Germany and UK where already have businesses
- All three are growing markets in services of at least 3% per year
- Assume additional $0.8m per country profit per year by 2018

> RIGHT NOW THIS SLIDE IS A DATA DUMP. NEED TO
> PRESENT INFORMATION VISUALLY IN ONE OR MORE SLIDES

Win three new contracts of at least $75m by 2018 and generate $2m incremental profit per year

- Solid pipeline of over 20 prospects with contract size at least $75m
- Sales team believe they can deliver at least 3 × $75m contracts
- Historical profit on such contracts was 5% per year based on four year average = $75m ÷ 4 × 0.04 = $0.93m per contract per year
- Some new pressures on profitability which are estimated to reduce profits by up to 30%
- Assume impact as $0.93m per contract per year, reduced by 30% to $0.66m per contract per year

> RIGHT NOW THIS SLIDE IS A DATA DUMP. NEED TO
> PRESENT INFORMATION VISUALLY IN ONE OR MORE SLIDES

Create easy to navigate webshop to deliver $1.3m

- Desire expressed in customer interviews to automate orders and to be able to place orders 24/7
- Survey of customers suggests that 80% of small and medium business could go online within three years and 40% of large business
- Significant growth of competitors with good webshops e.g. Technology Partners
- Higher spend per medium/small customer of around 10% where good webshop
- Risk of losing small and medium customers altogether with no decent webshop
- Significant costs estimated at $2m to build, with build time of six months
- Assume will achieve higher spend per customer, could be 10% but estimate 5% to be prudent
- Need to start build asap to not lose opportunity

> RIGHT NOW THIS SLIDE IS A DATA DUMP. NEED TO PRESENT INFORMATION VISUALLY IN ONE OR MORE SLIDES

Offer cradle to grave recycling services to deliver $1.2m incremental profit

- Recycling legislation in Europe and Canada already in place
- Recycling legislation arriving in US in 2018
- Feedback suggests existing customers just want this solved—meaning requirement for one-stop shop for recycling services
- Need to make process very simple and pain-free to ensure adoption
- Few offerings available today in USA
- Assume can win $20k per year of recycling services with 50 customers by 2018 = $1m revenue per year
- 10% of original value of approximately 40% equipment can be made by reselling it to metal traders
- Revenue from metal traders, assuming 2018 original value $0.5m per customer, 50 customers = $25m equipment, at 30% = $7.5m of equipment, sold at 10% = $0.75m
- Cost to deliver services = 6 people x $100k salary = $600k
- Estimated profit per year by 2018 = $1m + $0.75m - $0.6m = $1.2m

> RIGHT NOW THIS SLIDE IS A DATA DUMP. NEED TO PRESENT INFORMATION VISUALLY IN ONE OR MORE SLIDES

Cost-savings share model hypothesis was rejected

- Without more concrete thoughts on how to manage risk, cash outlay required makes this a non-starter
- Customers like the concept because it reduces their risk
- It's incredibly hard to determine what cost savings come as a result of this and what savings are the result of something else
- Even when this can be measured, savings take time to transpire
- Contrast this with large upfront costs for equipment, which would be a big drain on ITC cash flow

Slow-moving stock hypothesis was also rejected

- Lots of online platforms where can sell slow-moving stock
- Require up to the minute data and feeds to interface effectively with such platforms
- Cost to buy technology for this likely to be in region of $2m
- More detailed estimates suggest cost saving more like $0.3m per year as current sell off of slow-moving stock already includes some of this original $1m

Recommended combination of options are modularized services, webshop, new contracts and overseas sales team to yield $9.6m

Confirmed hypothesis	Estimated impact	Ease of implementation
F. Modularized services	$3.9m or $2.1m	Medium
A. Overseas sales teams	$2.4m	Medium
D. New contracts	$2.0m	High
E. Webshop	$1.2m	Low/Medium
C. Recycling	$1.2m	Medium/High

Combinations to deliver $8m:

- F_E, E, A, D = $9.6m   RECOMMENDED
- F_E, E, A, C = $8.8m
- F_E, E, D, C = $8.4m

Insufficient:

- E, A, D, C = $7.7m
- A, D, F, C = $6.9m

FROM STORYBOARD TO D$_4$ECIDE DOCUMENT

Once you have the presentation sketched out, turn your storyboard into formatted slides to give you the full presentation of recommended options: your D$_4$ecide Document.

For many of the slides in the example ITC storyboard above, further work would need to be done to translate the text on the body of the slide into charts and visuals so that the presentation is not just lots of text—that is the Design part of TOADS, plus adding Sources.

Don't forget to refer to the formatting guidelines in chapter 2.1 (from page 114) and take time to make them look good, so your audience can focus on the content. One way to do that is to ensure clean, consistent and non-distracting formatting.

Once TOADS has been implemented, do a final check to ensure that each slide has a clear title articulated as a "so what" and is articulating one message. Remember, you want to have drawn out all the inferences for the audience so your audience doesn't have to sit there and try to connect the dots themselves.

You may want to include an executive summary upfront, effectively your story written at the highest level in a handful of bullets. This enables the audience to understand straightaway what you will be sharing, as per the example below:

Executive summary

- Corporate plan for 2018 of $42m profit leaves us $8m short of $50m goal
- Need to ensure can deliver plan through winning renewals and extending existing customers
- In addition, four initiatives can close the $8m gap:
  - **Modularized Services:** Decouple our existing services package and provide flexible à la carte choice of service to deliver $3.9m
  - **Overseas sales team:** Build up teams in Canada, Germany and UK with prime focus on existing customers in US with operations in these countries to yield $2.4m
  - **New contracts beyond these assumed in plan:** Win three new contracts of at least $75m and $2m profit per year
  - **Webshop:** Create easy to navigate webshop to deliver $1.3m

---

With your D$_4$ecide Document in place, be sure there is ample time to debate it. You want to get to a place where is complete clarity about the choices you are recommending and why, where the are differing views you can work these through using FLIRT as your assessment tool, moving to alignment behind the choices.

Once your choices have been debated and alignment reached you are ready to move to the second part of D$_4$ecide: documenting your strategy.

D₄ECIDE CHECKLIST

- Choices are made after having reviewed all confirmed hypotheses.

- The chosen combination of options are balanced and are chosen to optimize what works best together.

- All key "so whats" are included in your storyline.

- The key points of your storyline together form a clear and simple story, which you could tell a child.

- The storyline has been faithfully translated into a storyboard.

- All information in the resulting presentation is relevant and required to meet the objectives and address the audience's needs or concerns.

- Knowing that on average it takes two minutes to present one slide, the number of slides you have matches the time you have for your presentation.

4.2

WRITE YOUR STRATEGY

"The ability to express an idea is well nigh as important as the idea itself."

Bernard Baruch

Strategy in 5D

Step	Chapter	Actions
D$_1$efine	1.1 Define Your Goal	Articulate goal as question ↓ Brainstorm sub-questions ↓
	1.2 Map Your Domain	Structure sub-questions
D$_2$iagnose	2.1 Diagnose Your Situation	Gather facts ↓ Draw insights ↓ Share findings
D$_3$evelop	3.1 Generate Hypotheses	Develop hypotheses ↓ Gather evidence ← Repeat until hypotheses confirmed or disproved
	3.2 Test Hypotheses	Draw insights ↓ Share findings
D$_4$ecide	4.1 Make Choices	Review combinations ↓ Debate scenarios ↓
	4.2 Write Your Strategy	**Document Choices**
D$_5$eliver	5.1 Communicate Your Strategy	Communicate strategy ↓ Pilot approach ↓
	5.2 Deliver Results	Adapt approach ↓ Track progress
ARC at every step		

KEY IDEAS

Strategy is the sum of your choices. With alignment behind your choices, you not only have all the core tenets of your strategy, but also the buy-in for these choices, and hence for your strategy.

Contrast this with having designed a strategy involving little collaboration. You may have put in tremendous effort, developed fantastic, rigorously researched ideas and translated all of this into an elegantly written strategy, but if this is your key stakeholders' first real glimpse of the strategy, their focus is unlikely to be on how to make the strategy work but on understanding and questioning your work and voicing where their views differ. Earlier in the process, differing views are crucial to sharpen and strengthen your thinking and in steps D_1, D_2 and D_3, these can be easily incorporated. Beyond the first part of step D_4ecide, however, where choices have been made, this simply does not work. Serious input received at this stage, which questions or unpicks choices, can be enough to throw the strategy off track.

Since you have been rigorously collaborative in your approach, you are now in a position where the strategy is a natural corollary of the buy-in and trust you have built. That means you can focus on the next critical task: accurately documenting your strategy.

As part of each step of Strategy in 5D, you are used to documenting and communicating your findings and that has been part of your work in each chapter. As we move to the end of the fourth step D_4ecide, we go further and dedicate this chapter to the documentation of your findings, that is, your Strategy in 5D Document.

It is hard to overestimate the importance of articulating your strategy precisely and clearly. As your strategy emerges based on choices made as part of D_4ecide, the resulting Strategy in 5D Document will form the basis of what you are doing—and what is understood about what your organization is doing—for the years to come. Your Strategy in 5D Document does not need to rehash all the reasons for getting to your choices although it is important to provide a synthesis of your outcomes for each of D_1efine, D_2iagnose, D_3evelop and D_4ecide.

Given the importance of the Strategy in 5D Document, it is imperative to get the wording precise, especially for the articulation of the strategy statement. So spend time on the wording, asking for feedback and revising it until it is clear.

Unlike all chapters since you developed your D_1efine Question Tree in chapter 1.2, our starting point is not the related sub-questions since there are no sub-questions on our tree dedicated to how we write our strategy - but instead we work from first principles with the following inputs and outputs that should underpin any Strategy in 5D Document. There are three key inputs:

What: Unambiguous written articulation of the organization's future actions. Clear delineation of what is part of the organization's strategy and what is not.

Impact: A set of measurable goals and a timeframe for delivery.

Needs: An overview of the key requirements and enablers to deliver the strategy.

Resulting from your Strategy in 5D Document, you also want two key outputs:

Decision-making framework: That enables staff of all levels who have read the strategy to be able to determine whether their own or their team's actions are—or are not—in service of the strategy, and then continue or discontinue these actions accordingly.

Communications document: A playbook for communication of the strategy for everyone in your organization and beyond. You need to be precise and informative as well as paint a goal and vision that inspires action.

WIN can be further broken down into the building blocks of the strategy:

What

1. **Mission:** A restatement or a revised version of your organization's mission, which provides an overarching holder for the strategy and which the strategy is aligned to.
2. **Strategy statement:** Concise articulation of where you are today, where you plan to get to and the key actions you have chosen to pursue to get there.
3. **Choices:** Decisions that comprise the strategy, described in detail including FLIRT assessment and the investment, resources and any other enablers that are required to deliver each.

Impact

4. **Sequencing:** The order, timing and interdependencies in the implementation of the choices.
5. **Financial impact:** The profit that this strategy will yield projected over time.
6. **Investment:** What investment is required, over what time period, and what the payback period will be.

Needs

7. **Enablers:** What is required to deliver the choices individually and overall including staff, skills, systems and structure, what gaps this reveals and how the enablers will change current operations.
8. **Governance:** How the delivery will be overseen including who will responsible for future decisions relating to the strategy and what the structures, roles, forums and processes will be to guide, navigate and as appropriate adapt the implementation of the strategy.
9. **Milestones:** The quantitative and qualitative measures you can put in place to track and assess your progress in implementing the choices and in moving towards your goal.

To best illustrate what a Strategy in 5D Document looks like, this chapter comprises a description of the different sections of the document, and provides examples of each for ITC.

DELIVERABLES, CONCEPTS, ARC AND MEETINGS

Step	Chapter	Key Concepts	Deliverables
D$_4$ecide	4.2 Write Your Strategy	What Impact Needs	Strategy in 5D document

Examples of application of ARC for documenting your strategy are:

- The written strategy includes a high-level implementation plan which is **actionable**
- The **rigorous** thinking behind the strategy is reflected in how it is written.
- To ensure that the strategy is accurately and clearly represented, feedback is sought on the documentation and wording of the strategy with **collaborative** input both from those who have been intensely involved and those who are new to the strategy.

The key meetings required to complete this chapter are:

- Strategy design team:
  - To carefully review Strategy in 5D Document, before sending to steering committee. Can be done in part via email.
- Steering committee:
  - Meeting to review articulation of the strategy, confirm any remaining details and sign it off, including investment.

Let's begin by looking at the three main components of **What**—mission, strategy statement and choices.

1. MISSION

In step **D₂iagnose** you reviewed your organization's current mission statement and values. Now is the time to return to these and make changes if required. If you don't have a mission statement or a written set of values, then this is a good time to create them. Remember to do this is collaboratively, by scheduling specific strategy design team meeting(s) to design and come up with a suggested mission and values that you can then review with the steering committee.

In some cases you will need to refine or add to them to ensure the encompass the new strategy without there being any sense of dissonance or misalignment. For example, suppose our strategy for ITC included a move into Asia, then the mission statement would need to be revised as follows:

> **Current ITC Mission:** To be North America and Europe's partner of choice for provision of IT products and services.

> **Revised ITC Mission:** To be North America, Europe and Asia's partner of choice for provision of IT products and services.

Typically I include the mission statement and values—including any proposed revisions—as the first page (excluding title page, contents, objectives etc.) of my Strategy in 5D Document. You can find what you would include for ITC here on page 117 of chapter 2.1.

2. STRATEGY STATEMENT

You need to be able to express your strategy in a very clear, precise and easy to understand way. Choose your wording carefully and test it with different audiences, including those who have not been involved in the strategy to date, to remove any ambiguities or gaps.

Overleaf is an articulation of ITC's strategy, including the articulation of starting and end points and includes the work on key account growth and renewals, which is required to deliver the corporate plan (initiative 1), plus the combination of the four options F_E, E, A and D, which are relabeled 2 through 5:

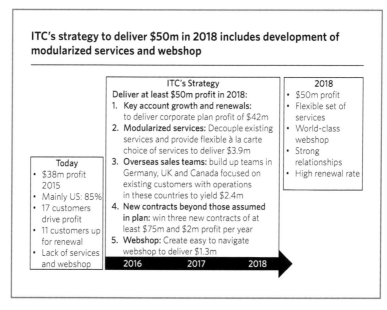

ITC's strategy to deliver $50m in 2018 includes development of modularized services and webshop

	ITC's Strategy Deliver at least $50m profit in 2018:	2018
	1. **Key account growth and renewals:** to deliver corporate plan profit of $42m	• $50m profit • Flexible set of services
	2. **Modularized services:** Decouple existing services and provide flexible à la carte choice of services to deliver $3.9m	• World-class webshop
Today • $38m profit 2015 • Mainly US: 85% • 17 customers drive profit • 11 customers up for renewal • Lack of services and webshop	3. **Overseas sales teams:** build up teams in Germany, UK and Canada focused on existing customers with operations in these countries to yield $2.4m	• Strong relationships • High renewal rate
	4. **New contracts beyond those assumed in plan:** win three new contracts of at least $75m and $2m profit per year	
	5. **Webshop:** Create easy to navigate webshop to deliver $1.3m	
	2016 2017 2018	

3. CHOICES THAT COMPRISE YOUR STRATEGY

You then want to detail your choices in turn. For each you want to include a description of the initiative and then a detailed FLIRT assessment including:

F Expected financial impact by year and investment required.

L Any dependencies on other choices or other support or initiatives in the organization.

I Ease of implementation and enablers to deliver.

R Risks and how these will be mitigated, including through other choices.

T Any comments on how the choice will fit and bit sequenced will other choices.

The following five slides describe each of the five initiatives for ITC, the first being what's required to deliver the corporate plan of $42m profit and the next four those chosen as the optimal combination to deliver the remaining $8m profit. You will note that these slides are much more developed than those in the choices storyboard from page 236, reflecting the detail required to ensure each initiative is actionable.

Corporate plan: Win renewals to main contract bases and grow six key accounts

Owner TBC

Name	Due up next three years	Profit 2015 ($m)
Spectrum	Y	4.1
Handy Andys	Y	2.9
Bellview Hotels	Y	2.1
Johnsons and Co	N	1.9
Advantage	Y	1.5
Decorum	Y	1.3
Furniture World	N	1.2
Ashton Breweries	Y	1.2
Kirkton and Jameson	Y	1.2
Alexander Enterprises	N	1.1
Infinitum	Y	1.1
Generation X	N	1.1
Experience Holidays	N	1.1
Spotlight	Y	1.1
Excalibur	Y	1.1
Wainwright	N	1.0
Younier Games	Y	1.0
Contracts due next 3 yrs	11	
Total		18.6

- **Key accounts:** Need to grow six contracts not up for renewal, by 9% per year.
- **Renewals:** Need to increase overall revenue for renews by 3% per year, with no overall losses. Any contract losses need to have profit at least replaced.

Projected financials by year			
	2016	2017	2018
Revenue	$1.3m	$1.3m	$1.4m
Opex	$0m	$0m	$0m
Profit	$1.3m	$1.3m	$1.4m

Key assumption: Use existing resources so no incremental cost

---

Modularized services: Decouple our existing services packages and provide flexible à la carte choice of services

Owner TBC

Projected financials by year				Key Assumptions
	2016	2017	2018	
Revenue	$0.2	$1.5m	$4.15m	- 20% rise in medium businesses and doubling in small businesses (to 2% overall).
Opex	$0.27	$0.26	$0.25	- Design can be done by in-house marketing team.
Profit (pre depreciation)	($0.07)	$1.2m	$3.9m	- Advertising/promotions budget at $250k pa; - Additional advertising budget: 2016: $20k, 2017: $10k, 2018: $0
Capex	$0	$0	$0	- Revenue dependent on creation of webshop by latest end Q1 2017

Staff	Skills	Systems	Structure
- Second two of services design team - No new recruits	- Develop skills in innovation and in translating customer needs into services	- No new systems required to support - Dependent on webshop to market	- Create modularized services design lead, reporting into services director

Overseas sales teams in Canada, Germany and the UK and target existing customers with operations in these countries

Owner
TBC

Projected financials by year					Key assumptions
	2015	2016	2017	2018	
Revenue					• Will build organically; no business we could buy in these countries gives us what we need
• Canada	$29m	$34m	$40m	$46m	
• Germany	$16m	$19m	$25m	$31m	• Assume one head per country, $250k
• UK	$18m	$23m	$28m	$34m	• Assume start with six sales staff per region, fully loaded cost of $120k each, increasing to 10 and then 12
Total Revenue	$63m	$76m	$93m	$111m	
Gross margin (12%)	$7.6m	$9.1m	$11.2m	$13.3m	• Assume 4 admin staff per country, cost of $75k each, rising to 8 and then 9
Current opex	$3.0m	$3.0m	$3.0m	$3.0m	• Assume office lease budget of $150k per year
Incremental opex	n/a	$1.7m	$3m	$3.4m	• Assume travel and entertainment budget of further $250k/country pa
Total profit	$4.5m	$4.4m	$5.2m	$6.9m	• Assume IT equipment, licenses and support $50k per year
Incremental profit	n/a	($0.1m)	$0.6m	$2.4m	• No capex

New contracts: Win three new contracts of at least $75m and $2m profit per year

Owner
TBC

- Currently pursuing eight potential new contracts
- Will be more contracts issued over next three years
- Need to win at least one big one of $75m per year
- We currently have seven that are more than $75m in size
- Recruit one expert bid writer at $120k fully loaded per year
- Introduce rigorous bid review process for leadership team and others to contribute to bid while it is being written and to rehearse for pitches
- Projected to yield $2m profit

Create easy to navigate webshop to deliver $1.3m

Owner TBC

Projected financials by year				Key Assumptions
	2016	2017	2018	• Build will cost of $2m
Revenue	$0	$0.4m	$1.3m	• Can be completed by end Q1 2017 (build time six months; need to
Opex	$0	$0.3m	$0.3m	select provider and plan what really want)
Cost savings	$0	$0.15m	$0.3m	• To maintain webshop need three system administrators at cost of
Profit (pre depreciation)	$0	$0.3m	$1.3	$75k each • Use existing call center team to handle calls and emails from
Capex	$2m			webshop customers • Systems running costs are $100k per year

4. SEQUENCING

You want to think about the timing for the roll-out each initiative in a way that reflects any interdependencies and that is also a realistic number of things to roll out at any one point in time, especially where multiple initiatives may draw on the same resource.

Break each initiative down into different steps of what needs to be delivered and list each of these down into the different tasks that need to be delivered and in order (with some quite possibly being in parallel) along with timing for each.

A good way to represent this visually is in a Gantt chart, which was developed by Henry Gantt in the 1910s. It is used in business and for major infrastructure projects (past projects include the Hoover Dam and the US Interstate highway system). It visually lays out workstreams and timings, as per the following example:

The five initiatives would be sequenced over three years

Initiative	Workstream	
1. Key account growth and renewals	Ensure sales teams understand goals	
	Instigate new bid review procedures	
	Ongoing delivery of goals	
2. Modularized services	Identify which services should be sold à la carte	
	Determine pricing for these services	
	Design marketing and copy for website	
	Hire marketing agency to run promotion campaign	
	Conduct customer interviews to identify needs	
3. Overseas sales teams	Recruit country heads for each country	
	Recruit sales teams: first wave	
	Recruit admin staff: first wave	
	Find premises and set up logistics	
	Recruit sales teams: second wave	
	Recruit admin staff: second wave	
4. New contracts	Recruit new bid manager	
	Make pipeline system more rigorous	
	Put in place pipeline reviews	
	Ensure win at least one contract per year	
5. Webshop	Determine key features of webshop and write spec	
	Have beauty parade of providers and select one	
	Build	
	Ongoing management and maintenance	

	2016				2017				2018			
	Q1	Q2	Q3	Q4	Q1	Q2	Q3	Q4	Q1	Q2	Q3	Q4
	■											
		■										
			■	■	■	■	■	■	■			
		■										
		■										
			■									
				■	■							
						■	■	■	■	■	■	■
	■	■										
		■	■									
		■										
			■	■								
							■	■				
	■											
		■										
			■									
	■	■	■	■	■	■	■	■	■	■	■	■
	■											
		■										
			■	■	■							
						■	■	■	■	■	■	■

5. FINANCIAL IMPACT

Here you want to show a complete picture of the financial impact of the strategy, both overall and broken down by initiative.

Five key initiatives, including corporate plan, to deliver additional $13.6m profit from 2015's $38m and $9.6m beyond corporate plan

Initiative	Estimated Impact	Ease of implementation	
1. Corporate plan	$4.0m	Medium	
2. Modularized services	$3.9m	Medium	
3. Overseas sales teams	$2.4m	Medium	$9.6m
4. New contracts	$2.0m	High	
5. Webshop	$1.3m	Low/Medium	
Collectively	$13.6m	Medium	

A good way to represent the summary financial information visually is in a waterfall chart that maps the profit today against desired profit and shows what each initiative will contribute financially to meeting that goal.

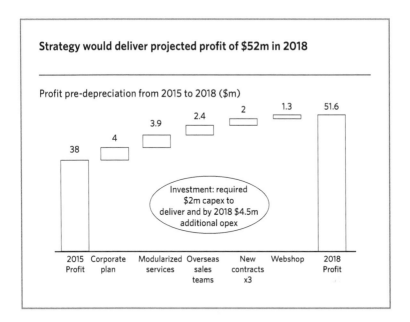

Strategy would deliver projected profit of $52m in 2018

Profit pre-depreciation from 2015 to 2018 ($m)

Investment: required $2m capex to deliver and by 2018 $4.5m additional opex

38	4	3.9	2.4	2	1.3	51.6
2015 Profit	Corporate plan	Modularized services	Overseas sales teams	New contracts x3	Webshop	2018 Profit

6. INVESTMENT

Layout a timeline of the upfront and ongoing investment required to deliver the initiatives. This should reflect the sequencing of the initiatives and display the payback period for the investments.

Also highlight where cash is needed versus where profit from the initiatives can be used to fund the required investments.

Investment of over $5m required with no payback more than 3 years

Initiative	Estimated impact	Investment required	Timing	Payback (years)
1. Corporate plan	$4.0m	0 to $400k	Annual	2
2. Modularized services	$3.9m	0		0
3. Overseas sales team	$2.4m	$1.7m to $3.4m	Starts	3
4. New contracts	$2.0m	$120k		1.5
5. Webshop	$1.3m	$2m one-off + $325k ongoing		Low/ medium
Collectively	$13.6m			Medium

7. ENABLERS

Here you want to think about what is required to enable the strategy overall including:

- **Staff:** what new and existing staff will be required.
- **Skills:** what existing skills must be developed and what additional skills are required.
- **Systems:** both IT and operational processes required to be successful.
- **Structure:** any required organizational changes e.g. new reporting lines[27]
- Where appropriate, sales and marketing approach and key customer targets.
- Whether what's required can be realized organically or will need to be delivered through acquisition, or a combination of the two.

Key enablers for delivering the strategy include sufficient skilled sales staff plus technology skills to deliver the webshop

Skills	• Skilled sales staff in US to sell new modularized services • Also lighter sales model to reach medium sized companies	Systems	• Need flexible and rigorous testing approach for webshop while in development to ensure to deliver what customers want
Staff	• Hiring of sales staff in Canada, UK and Germany - or acquisition of organization with strong sales staff	Structure	• Need to create appropriate structure in each of Canada, UK and Germany

---

8. GOVERNANCE

It is critical to put in place good governance to manage and review progress in implementing the initiatives. No doubt, things that you hadn't thought of will come up or things won't turn out how you expected and it is important to be able to have others around to best advise your course of action.

Good governance also holds people to account. You have not made all this effort to have a strategy sit in a drawer and not be implemented. All individuals or groups involved in governance should ensure that milestones set clearly, and then that they are met, and if they are not, enquire why they are not being met and what needs to be done in response.

Finally, good governance should provide a forum for learning: if you can understand what has worked well and why, and what has worked less well and why, then everyone gains important lessons not just for the remaining implementation but also for all sorts of other future situations.

For this to be effective, it requires an environment that allows those involved in implementation to share successes and mistakes equally and for them to be received in an open, curious way, rather than with any sense of only wanting to hear good news. Nor should you share mistakes as a way to reprimand someone. As soon as that happens just once, you can forget about hearing honest feedback. Not that people should never be reprimanded, but this cannot take place in a meeting where you are inviting people to share openly.

There are various ways in which to provide the desired governance. One approach can be to use the steering committee that designed the strategy as an oversight committee, who can help you keep on track by meeting every quarter.

You may also want to have a Delivery Office who take on a more formal responsibility for governance and delivery. We will talk more about this in chapter 5.2.

Whether you have a Delivery Office or not, you are likely to want an operational level committee who meet at least once a month.

Proposed governance includes delivery team reviewing progress each month and steering committees quarterly

	Purpose	Frequency
Steering committee	• Review progress against milestones • Discuss any big changes/surprises to what expected • Agree any significant change to plan	• Quarterly • Papers submitted in advance
Delivery team review	• Review progress against milestones • Review detailed operations on each initiative, with all initiative owners to present • Discuss any big changes/surprises to what expected • Agree any minor changes; any major changes should be recommended to strategy steering committee for approval (no need to wait for meeting; email request or additional meeting)	• Monthly

Make sure you create a culture of accountability for the meetings. For example, there should be a clear set of actions—with tasks delegated to owners—coming out of each operational committee. This should be systematically reviewed at the following meeting and there should be no excuses for not having completed actions, or else the meeting risks becoming a talking shop rather than a vehicle for getting things done. At this stage, you also want to start thinking about owners for each of the key initiatives underpinning your strategy, plus owners for any functional areas like IT or HR that span across multiple initiatives. We will return to this in chapter 5.2.

9. MILESTONES

For each initiative you want to define upfront milestones for each year of the strategy. These include meeting the financial goals, but also other goals around development and the launch of new products or services and hiring of new staff or development of new skills.

2016 milestones have been set for each initiative

Initiative	2016 overall
1. Corporate plan	• $1.3m incremental profit • Growth in at least two of six targeted key accounts • Renewal of six accounts and to contract base equivalent to at least previous total
2. Modularized services	• New services designed and launched • Advertising program in place to extend into 2017 • Breakeven financially, does not exceed $300k incremental costs • On course to make $1.2m incremental profit in 2017
3. Overseas sales teams	• New head of business in place in each Canada, Germany and UK • Six new sales staff and four new admin staff in each of three countries • Breakeven financially, do not exceed $300k incremental costs • On course to make $0.6m incremental profit in 2017
4. New contracts	• Win at least one new contract of at least $75m and add new bid writer • Rigorous bid review process in place
5. Webshop	• Webshop at least 80% and ready to launch in Q1 2017 • Full build costs not to exceed $2m

---

With your Strategy in 5D Document assembled, now spend time testing it, primarily with stakeholders, so that it becomes refined and ready for the first part of our final step D_5eliver: Communicating the launch of your strategy.

STRATEGY IN 5D DOCUMENT CHECKLIST

You have a Strategy in 5D Document which includes:

- A clear and concise articulation of the initiatives that make up the strategy.

- Sufficient detail on each initiative to know financial projections and key enablers.

- The financial goals and expected impact.

- The sequencing and interdependencies of the initiatives that comprise the strategy.

- How progress will be reviewed and managed (milestones and governance).

D$_1$efine

D$_2$iagnose

D$_3$evelop

D$_4$ecide

D$_5$eliver

5.1

COMMUNICATE YOUR STRATEGY

*"Communication is about getting others
to adopt your point of view, to help them
understand why you're excited. If all you want
to do is create a file of facts and figures, then
cancel the meeting and send in a report."*

Seth Godin

Strategy in 5D

Step	Chapter	Actions
D$_1$efine	1.1 Define Your Goal	Articulate goal as question ↓ Brainstorm sub-questions ↓
	1.2 Map Your Domain	Structure sub-questions
D$_2$iagnose	2.1 Diagnose Your Situation	Gather facts ↓ Draw insights ↓ Share findings
D$_3$evelop	3.1 Generate Hypotheses	Develop hypotheses ↓ Gather evidence ↩ Repeat until hypotheses confirmed or disproved
	3.2 Test Hypotheses	Draw insights ↓ Share findings
D$_4$ecide	4.1 Make Choices	Review combinations ↓ Debate scenarios ↓
	4.2 Write Your Strategy	Document choices
D$_5$eliver	5.1 Communicate Your Strategy	Communicate strategy ↓ Pilot approach ↓
	5.2 Deliver Results	Adapt approach ↓ Track progress
ARC at every step		

KEY IDEAS

You have done a tremendous amount of work to get here. You are in an exciting place—and yet too many times I have heard about beautiful, thought-through strategy documents never leaving the manager's desk drawer. You need to be vigilant and keep adhering to the ARC principles since the transition from finalized choices to successful delivery of these choices, is the most challenging part of Strategy in 5D, where things can easily go wrong. .

Your first task is to communicate your strategy to your broader set of stakeholders, who will likely be eagerly (and sometimes anxiously) waiting to hear what has been decided. You do not want to procrastinate in communicating your decisions and the resulting strategy to them—if you leave a communications vacuum, rumors will fill the space, leading to anxiety and a loss of focus and motivation.

How well you communicate the strategy will have big implications. A staff who understand and are motivated by the strategy will make all the difference to the how skillfully the strategy is delivered and the will and hard work that people are willing to put into delivering it. Simply put, if you can't get the people who need to deliver the strategy on your side, then you are going to struggle to deliver the strategy.

You are likely to have three core audiences to address with your strategy: the steering committee (who are included here for completeness, but who should have already been communicated to), the wider staff and your external audience including investors, customers and suppliers.

For each audience, you want to define what you want the outcome of each meeting to be, and whether that means you will need to inform your audience, engage them in the strategy or whether you actually want to discuss it with them. (This is analogous to how you prepare for any meeting, as we discussed in chapter 1.1).

With the steering committee, you are sharing a strategy based on choices they have already agreed. You will likely have added more detail on the financials, sequencing, milestones and governance and you want there to be time to discuss these—but not to rehash decisions already made.

With staff, you want to first think about whether to segment them into groups for communication purposes. For example, you may want to segment your audience by seniority, with those who are middle or senior managers briefed in advance of a presentation to all staff so that they are prepared to answer questions from their staff.

In terms of your purpose when presenting to staff, you are essentially informing them of the strategy. If there are staff whose input and feedback you would like on the strategy, then that is quite different and needed to have happened much earlier in the Strategy in 5D process. What matters here is the intent and tone you create for the presentation—and these are quite different if you want input. If you are at a stage where you are no longer actively looking for input on the design of the strategy, you can be genuinely receptive and thoughtful about any input received, but do not set any expectations about incorporating it.

While your intent and tone is one of informing people about the strategy, you may actively want to encourage input on how it will be delivered. This will likely give you a richer set of ideas and help you with buy-in for the hard work ahead, implementing your strategy.

With any external audience at this stage your task will be to inform in a way that shows relevance to their needs. As with staff, if you want views from colleagues external to the organization then that needs to happen earlier during steps D_2iagnose and D_3evelop.

Your Strategy in 5D Document will be helpful as your think about what you want to say to each audience - but do not start there. It is better to step back and for each audience write a storyline that addresses their needs and what you need to convey. Ultimately this will likely draw on several slides from your Strategy in 5D Document—but the crucial difference is if your start with your storyline you will generate the right messages and flow versus a presentation that feels like a patchwork quilt made of slides of one or more other presentations. This point is a general one: when you are asked to make a presentation you may think it saves you time to pick slides from other presentation – and in the first 30 minutes it will seem to be so. But those 30 minutes spent mapping out your storyline and storyboard are invaluable and once you have your key messages and flow in place you are already a long way towards a strong presentation and will get there much faster.

All of us have had to sit through presentations that are poorly structured or contain badly written slides. If a presentation is hard going or there are things that are difficult for the audience to follow, you will quickly lose them. A lost audience means there is no chance of them leaving feeling inspired or excited to talk strategy with colleagues, let alone wanting to mention it to the CEO the next time he or she asks what important things are going on.

No matter who your audience is, a key skill is to keep your objectives front and center in your mind, both while preparing the presentation and during delivery. Then, regardless of surprises— for example, you receive a set of unexpected questions that take you off course—you can tailor your response in a way that still enables you to meet your objectives.

When giving presentations and sharing information in a meeting, it is critical to develop a feel for time. You want to know how long each section of the presentation takes. Then, if for example, your time is halved, you can very quickly work out what to drop and what to keep. You also know how much time to allow for questioning that wanders off topic and when it is time to politely move on.

The location of meetings matters, for example it sends a different message if you make people come to you, versus if you go to them. Think also about the environment and the setting in which you will be presenting, as it makes a big difference to how people feel and behave. You don't always have a choice in this but when you do, you want to think about the type of room and layout that will best create the atmosphere you want. Also, be sure to have the technology and props you need, such as a projector, whiteboard, flipcharts and/or video conferencing, and if you are not familiar with the room, test it all works beforehand. There is nothing worse than having done all this work only to be hampered in your delivery by technology not working as it should.

To bring all this together, you want to create a comms plan for the launch of your strategy that also includes the timing of each of the meetings with each audience. You should do this collaboratively with the strategy design team and with input from stakeholders to ensure no audience is missed and any potentially tricky meetings can be well thought through. There is often sequencing as to who should come first. You should also think about if you want the same person/people to present or if you will vary that based on the audience.

Really, this phase prior to delivering your presentation is about being as prepared as you can be, so you are ready for every surprise.

DELIVERABLES, CONCEPTS, ARC AND MEETINGS

Step	Chapter	Key Concepts	Deliverables
D$_5$eliver	5.1 Communicate Your Strategy	Audience and their needs Desired outcomes	D$_5$eliver Launch Communications Plan

Examples of application of ARC for communicating the launch of your strategy are:

- The communications plan is **actionable** with clear owners and timing.
- The communications plan is **rigorously** thought through, with approaches tailored to each audience.
- The communications plan is created and reviewed **collaboratively** to ensure optimal messaging and no audience overlooked.

The key meetings required to complete this chapter are:

- Strategy design team:
  - Create communications plan for strategy launch
  - Deliver presentations.
- Steering committee:
  - Review communications plan for strategy launch
  - Discuss feedback from presentations.
  - Celebrate launch with strategy design team.

DEVELOPING YOUR LAUNCH COMMS PLAN

As with all the chapters since the introduction of the D_1efine Question Tree—bar the last one on writing your strategy—we start with the sub-questions related to this step and place them in a table, our D_5eliver Launch Communications Table.

D_5ELIVER LAUNCH COMMUNICATIONS TABLE						
Sub-questions						
7.1 Who needs to be communicated to?	Add each audience to a unique column, adding columns as necessary					
7.2 What is the purpose of the communication and the desired outcomes?	Answer per audience					
7.3 What does each audience need?	Answer per audience					
7.4 What medium should be used, how many meetings are required and where should they be?	Answer per audience					
7.5 Who should present, with what materials?	Answer per audience					
7.6 What is the timing?	Answer per audience					

Like the sub-questions for the fourth step D_4ecide, the sub-questions for ITC are not specific to ITC and similar sub-questions typically arise regardless of the organization or topic of focus.

Just as we used FLIRT in the fourth step D_4ecide to simplify answering questions, here I use a Communications Triangle, comprising of ten elements, which I use to complete my D_5eliver Launch Communications Table. The ten elements are grouped into three tiers: Who, What and How:

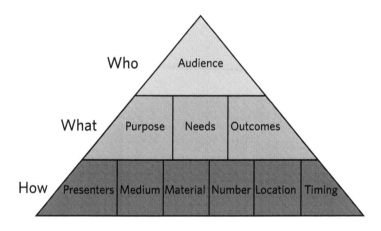

Figure 34: Communications Triangle

For ITC, the sub-questions correlate to these ten elements and so can replace the sub-questions on the D_5eliver Launch Communications Table.

The plan for communicating the launch of the strategy is, of course, only the start of the communications required for successful delivery of the strategy. As part of the implementation plan, you will need to have a communications workstream and determine how you will best update people on progress and keep them engaged long-term.

An example comms plan to launch ITC's strategy is overleaf after the D_5eliver Launch Communications Table opposite:

D₅ELIVER LAUNCH COMMUNICATIONS TABLE

Who

Audience Who are you communicating to?	Add each audience to a unique column		

What

Purpose Why are you communicating, e.g. to inform, to engage, to discuss?	Answer per audience		
Needs What will the audience be looking to have addressed?	Answer per audience		
Outcomes What you want the audience to know, feel and do as a result?	Answer per audience		

How

Presenter(s) Who will deliver it?	Answer per audience		
Medium How communication will take place to both inform the meeting is happening and then at the meeting itself?	Answer per audience		
Material What will be used at the meeting and provided in advance?	Answer per audience		
Number of meetings How many meetings to reach the audiences?	Answer per audience		
Location Where will the communications occur?	Answer per audience		
Timing How long will they take?	Answer per audience		

D5ELIVER LAUNCH COMMS PLAN			
Audience	Steering committee	Top 50 managers group	All staff
Purpose	• Share final strategy and discuss implementation • Get buy-in for strategy and its dissemination	• Share strategy • Impart their importance for input and for delivery • Hear any concerns	• Share strategy • Impart their importance to delivery • Hear any concerns
Outcomes	• Aligned and will help communicate strategy • Avoid re-discussing that already agreed	• Understand the strategy and supportive of it • Readiness to be able to talk to staff about it	• Understand the strategy • Supportive and enthusiastic about it
Need of audience	• Strategy reflects findings • Feel any concerns are addressed	• Understand if job is safe • Understand direction and what is expected	• Understand if job is safe • Understand direction and what is expected
Medium	• In person	• In person	• In person
Number	• 1	• 1	• 6
Location	Head office	Head office	SF, NY, LA, Miami, Austin, Chicago
Presenter(s)	• Strategy design team leader plus team members	• CEO • Strategy design leader	• CEO • Strategy design leader • Local senior staff
Material	• Strategy in 5D Document with appendices • Circulated in advance	• Strategy in 5D Document with appendices • Printout at meeting	• Strategy in 5D Document no appendices • Printed summary; no pre-read
Timing	Mar 7th	Mar 14th	Mar 15th to 18th

Investors	20 key accounts, plus any others interviewed	5 key suppliers plus any others interviewed
• To get them excited about the next phase of growth for the organization	• Thank them for input to strategy • Share benefits of the strategy • Hear any concerns	• Thank them for input to strategy • Explain requirements resulting from strategy
• Feel confident about their investment • Increase probability of future investments	• Keen to buy new services • Tell others about these	• Suppliers think about whether changes required
• To know their money is in good hands and is being used wisely	• Understand changes and what new services will be available	• Understand whether services still needed and in what capacity
• In person • Webcast	• Mix of in person, webcast and conf. calls	• Mix of in person, webcast and conf. calls
• 1 of each	>20	>4
In person = NY Webcast = n/a	Various, ideally customer sites	Various, ideally supplier's sites
• CEO; CFO	• Account manager(s) plus design team	• Account manager(s) plus design team members
• Strategy in 5D Document no appendices • Printed summary at meeting	• Strategy in 5D Document no appendices • Printed summary at meeting	• Strategy in 5D Document no appendices • Printed summary; no pre-read
Mar 21st and Mar 24th	Apr various	Apr various

PREPARING FOR EACH PRESENTATION

One of the most important things you can do when writing and giving a presentation is to put yourself in the shoes of the audience. This will give you an invaluable perspective and alert you to audience needs and concerns that may arise. It also helps tailor the precise language and tone of your presentation.

You should do this specifically for each audience and use what you see as a way to preempt likely questions and concerns. I often make a list of the questions I expect and then make notes about the answer I would give.

Other things to consider as you prepare include:

- **Provide plenty of notice for the meeting through multiple mediums.** Think about all the different ways to reach your audiences, for example posting material on the company intranet or posting flyers in offices.
- **Be explicit about the purpose of the presentation upfront,** in the invite to the meeting and again at the begin of the meeting.
- **Set up a pre-meeting** if you are particularly concerned about an audience member's response or where it is critical to have their support at the presentation. Use it to run through the presentation and be able to address any concerns privately.
- **Plan your presentation in carefully timed blocks,** including time for questions and discussion—and be realistic about how long things will take.
- **Conduct a final review of your slides for typos and for superfluous words.** Every word counts, so if a word or phrase is not adding anything, cut it out.
- **Know your material** inside out so that you no longer really need your slides. This means you are much less likely to read verbatim from your slides and allows you to be more natural and fluid.
- **Do a dry-run,** even if only to yourself. Do it in the format you will be presenting, so if it will be on screen, practice the presentation on screen, not with a print out.

- **Check equipment before the presentation day.** This may sound trivial, but too many times I've seen equipment not work on the day and it can have devastating effects. It is likely to unnerve you and also means that people cannot actually see your findings.
- **Circulate any helpful pre-reading material.** Choose pre-reading carefully, you want the audience to be well-informed and able to think prior to the meeting, but you also do not want to provide partial information that inadvertently leads to misinterpretation or unhelpful chit-chat and rumor. When communicating a new strategy to an audience who have not been involved in its design, a pre-read usually does not make sense since it would likely lead to questions and risk of misinterpretation.

DELIVERING EACH PRESENTATION

It's the day of one of your presentations. Here are a few important things to do during the presentation:

- **Get yourself comfortable.** Don't rush to start. Be poised. Get a feel for the room and the audience. They are here to listen to you, and what you have to say is important.
- **Start with a proper introduction** and context to get everyone on the same page. You know why you are there, but the audience, in one of many meetings of their day, may not.
- **Avoid talking too fast,** which is easy to do if you are nervous. I sometimes write in the margins of my slides "don't talk too fast" as a reminder. You can also tell someone in the room about this and ask them to signal if you are talking too fast.
- **Find a friend**[28] and do so fast, meaning as you refer to something that you know is important to one of the audience members, verbally acknowledge the audience member and their viewpoint at the same time. For example, "Jane, I know you raised the need to balance strategy with more operations overseas and you'll see that we have incorporated this as an important part of the strategy." This will help engage the person and bring you an early ally. You can repeat this a few times with

different people especially if someone looks unengaged. It is a great way to bring them into the presentation.

- **Be sure to highlight the key message** of each slide and guide the audience through what they are looking at with each slide, but avoid reading verbatim. For example, "On the left you can see a bar chart showing profitability in Germany over the past three years. This shows stagnation in our profitability caused by... On the right you have quotes from some of our US customers who have operations in Germany but who we don't serve today. Of note is..."

- **Preempt likely questions or objections** to slides as you describe them. Suppose there have been concerns as to how to address recent customer feedback. You can preempt a lot of discussion by making a statement such as: "You might be wondering how this will help address the recent customer feedback we received. Well..." and then go on to explain how the strategy does this.

- **Add richness to your slides with examples and anecdotes.** I sometimes add Post-It® notes with examples on specific slides so I remember to talk about those examples when I am on the earmarked slide.

- **Be aware of the audience's body language** as this can reveal how much they are following and engaged and where they agree or disagree with what you're saying.

- **Allow space to receive comments or questions from the audience.** Remember, people are much more likely to be supportive if they feel their points are acknowledged and addressed.

- **Verbally check in with the audience every few slides,** asking if there are any questions on what has been presented so far. This is especially important if you are not getting many comments or questions.

- **State the slide number you are on** every couple of slides if you have people listening or watching remotely.

AVOIDING DERAILMENT

A big concern is what to do if the audience starts asking lots of questions that take you off topic. Do you answer them at the risk of not getting through your material, or do you move on, and when?

My advice would be to allow a few questions that are off topic. If they however continue, and you can see that you are going to run out of time, I suggest acknowledging each person who asks a question and the importance of their question and asking if you can continue another time. For example, "I'd love to discuss more of your questions, but I am conscious that we only have X minutes remaining. If we continue I am concerned that we won't get through the rest of the presentation which I think has some important ideas we should cover today. Would it be okay if we pause on the questions for this session and agree a follow-up session to discuss them in depth as soon as possible?"

HANDLING UNEXPECTED QUESTIONS

I am also often asked what to do if, despite good preparation, you are asked a question you are not prepared for and do not know the answer to.

If you get flustered, first re-center yourself, then take a couple of breaths and re-center yourself again before responding. Then, flustered or not, I do not advise trying to piece together an answer if you really don't know it. Better to acknowledge that it's an important question and that you'd like to think about it first or that you need to check a couple of pieces of information before responding. Then promise to get back to the person with the answer fast. Provide a timeframe for this and make sure you do follow-up in that timeframe. There is rarely anything that needs to absolutely be answered immediately. So in almost all cases, it is much better to have the right answer later than to have a guess in the moment.

D$_5$ELIVER LAUNCH COMMS CHECKLIST

- You have a communications plan for the launch of your strategy

- Your plan encompasses the first four elements of a good plan: identifying the audience and the purpose of your communication, plus desired outcomes and audience needs.

- Your plan also includes a further six elements: the medium for communication, how many meetings are needed, what material will be prepared and presented, the location, presenter(s) and timings

- You have spent time to prepare for presentations beyond writing slides, for example, checking out the room and planning the time allotted per section of the presentation.

- You have a good feel for your audience and their needs and concerns before you get in the room.

- You calibrate the storyline, insights and presentation for each audience, varying level of detail, complexity and length depending on the audience type and needs.

- You feel confident about what you will be presenting.

5.2

DELIVER RESULTS

"Without strategy, execution is aimless.
Without execution, strategy is useless."

Morris Chang

Strategy in 5D

Step	Chapter	Actions
D$_1$efine	1.1 Define Your Goal	Articulate goal as question ↓ Brainstorm sub-questions ↓
	1.2 Map Your Domain	Structure sub-questions
D$_2$iagnose	2.1 Diagnose Your Situation	Gather facts ↓ Draw insights ↓ Share findings
D$_3$evelop	3.1 Generate Hypotheses	Develop hypotheses ↓ Gather evidence
	3.2 Test Hypotheses	Repeat until hypotheses confirmed or disproved ↓ Draw insights ↓ Share findings
D$_4$ecide	4.1 Make Choices	Review combinations ↓ Debate scenarios ↓
	4.2 Write Your Strategy	Document choices
D$_5$eliver	5.1 Communicate Your Strategy	Communicate strategy ↓ Test plan
	5.2 Deliver Results	Adapt plan ↓ Track Progress

ARC at every step

KEY IDEAS

You have a strategy in place and you and your team have communicated it to all relevant parties. But if you can't deliver it, then it is not worth the paper it is written on.

The transition to delivering your strategy is delicate. Often the people in charge of delivering your strategy are not the same people who designed it. Knowledge held by the design team must be rigorously transferred to avoid thinking being lost, actions falling through the cracks or worse still, the strategy just not happening.

The transition to delivery also reminds us why ARC is such an important set of principles:

- Having made the strategy **actionable**, you avoid an otherwise inevitable hiatus in delivering it, or worse it never being delivered.
- By having **rigorously** documented the strategy you minimize gaps that would lead to oversights in delivery.
- Thanks to prior **collaboration** between those designing the strategy and those delivering it you avoid people saying "I never agreed with the strategy in the first place", which otherwise can carry a lot of unhelpful momentum.

A good starting point is to return to the "how" factors you identified when you were writing the Strategy in 5D Document:

- **Enablers:** what is required to deliver the choices individually and overall.
- **Governance:** how the delivery will be overseen.
- **Milestones:** the quantitative and qualitative measures you can put in place to track and assess the progress.

Your task is to translate these "hows" into the next level of detail—and continue to do this from now until the strategy is fully implemented. You do not need to be able to—nor would it be realistic—to map out every step that will need to be taken. What you do need is sufficient detail for what's required in the coming months and sufficient understanding of the overall direction to be able to add new steps as you learn more.

Begin by thinking through in more detail about the enablers required to deliver the strategy and what this means for responsibilities added to existing parts of the organization and what new skills and/or people will need to be added. For each area, what matters most are the differences from what you do or have today in each of these areas and what you will need to do to deliver each from today's starting points.

Once you have mapped out your enablers, you can look at what is required to align these into workstreams and also how these align with existing budgets and other plans such as technology plans.

This information should form part of a detailed D_5elivery plan. Typically, it should include one workstream for each key choice, plus one for each of the key functional areas, such as IT and HR, and one for each of governance and communication.

Assign owners for each of the workstreams. Work closely with all the initiative owners to ensure they understand the strategy and what is expected of them, and have what they need to succeed. Each owner should develop the detail on his or her initiative. The overall group of owners should also come together to collaboratively review all initiatives, what all the details add up to, making changes as appropriate to fill any gaps and ensure coherence.

Think of the D_5elivery plan as a dynamic, living document which should be regularly updated to document what has been done, what has been learned and what this all means when translated into future plans. This contrasts with the Strategy in 5D Document, which once written is fixed, bar any revisions—which are rare.

You may want to set up a Delivery Office to oversee the delivery of the strategy, particularly if there are many different parts of the organization involved in delivering the strategy. This ensures dedicated expertise on the "how to" and on the running of the governance to deliver the strategy, plus ensures sharing of best practice between initiatives.

The role of the Delivery Office can range from lighter touch co-ordination of workstreams (Delivery Coordinator) to a role that helps to plan and deliver the implementation (Delivery Director) or something in the middle (Delivery Manager). With either a Delivery Manager or Director, the role requires holding people to account for delivering the strategy and may therefore require initiative owners to have a dotted reporting line to the Delivery Director/Manager as well as the reporting line to their current manager.

Once you have your workstreams, owners and a decision on a Delivery Office, map out the milestones for each initiative and overall. You have a starting point for these milestones from your Strategy in 5D Document and now you add more details and tangibility. Include in this how you will pilot different aspects of each initiative and what you will be testing with the pilot and how pilot learnings will be fed into how the strategy is implemented overall.

I cannot emphasize enough the importance of being willing to try things and make mistakes—and of course, learn from them. However much we put the best brains to work when designing a strategy, no-one can foresee every instance or predict every change that requires subtle or not so subtle refinements to the strategy.

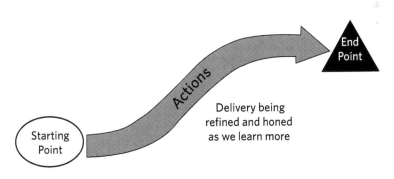

Figure 35: Navigating delivery to the desired end point

Effective metrics and governance not only ensures progress stays on track but also facilitates this culture of testing and piloting of each initiative, where changes to delivery are decided swiftly based on what is learned, and the final delivery is well honed and refined.

Then keep going! You are effectively testing, revising, implementing, testing some more, revising and implementing until your strategy is realized. As you learn, document this and the implications of your learnings for what you implement. If there are learnings backed with appropriate rigor that change the overall strategy then update your strategy, noting that you do not do this lightly. Updating your strategy is at most a once a year occurrence and often less frequent.

This chapter does comprehensively cover how to deliver a strategy and all the pitfalls and setbacks you may encounter —that would take another book. It provides important concepts and principles to incorporate into your delivery. Use them well and do not hesitate to read further in this area to support delivery of your strategy in the months and years ahead.

DELIVERABLES, CONCEPTS, ARC AND MEETINGS

Step	Chapter	Key Concepts	Deliverables
D$_5$eliver	5.2 Deliver Results	COST and ADAPT Governance and Delivery Office Piloting and Milestones	D$_5$elivery Workstreams Table D$_5$elivery Plan

Examples of application of ARC for delivering your strategy includes an implementation plan which is:

- **Actionable** with clear, unambiguous steps to be taken that any good manager would be able to follow.
- **Rigorous** with no gaps. Where you don't know what to do yet, rather than leaving a gap highlight this fact and work to fill it with colleagues.
- A **collaboratively** created living document which is regularly updated.

The key meetings required to complete this chapter are:

- Strategy design team:
  - Meet with initiative owners and Delivery Office (where it exists) to share details on each initiative, with ample time for those who will need to deliver to ask questions.
  - Many meetings with delivery owners and others until the strategy is fully delivered.
- Delivery team:
  - Too many to list. Delivering the strategy is an art and will require many meetings over months and years.

IDENTIFYING ENABLERS WITH "COST"

As with earlier chapters, we begin by returning to our D$_1$efine Question Tree for ITC and review the sub-questions related to this part of D$_5$eliver.

Put the related sub-questions into a table: the D_5elivery Information Table. In the columns of the table, add the choices which form the strategy:
1. Corporate plan
2. Modularized services
3. Overseas sales teams
4. New contracts
5. Webshop

D_5ELIVERY INFORMATION TABLE						
	1.	2.	3.	4.	5.	Overall
8.1 What needs to change in terms of how we reach and serve customers?			Add comments			
8.2 What needs to change in terms of offering?			Add comments			
8.3 What new skills are required, how much and where?			Add comments			
8.4 What technology is required and by when?			Add comments			
8.5 How does what's required translate into workstreams and align with existing plans?			List workstreams			
8.6 What is the role of the Delivery Office and/or other governance?			Add comments			
8.7 How can plans best be adapted and piloted and then revised accordingly for another round of testing?			Add comments			
8.8 How can progress best be tracked?			Add comments			

Like we have seen in earlier chapters, the sub-questions for ITC for this step are not ITC specific. The first four sub-questions refer to enablers of the strategy, questions five and six are about alignment and governance and the final two sub-questions are about piloting and tracking.

You can think about your enablers in terms of staff, skills, systems and structure, as referred to in chapter 4.2. As I get into greater levels of detail, I prefer to think of the four areas of enablers by using the acronym **COST** and you can use the work you have done already on staff, skills, systems and structure to overlay with COST:

C **ustomer:** How you will reach and serve your customers to deliver your strategy and what needs to change to do this.

O **ffering:** What you will be offering to customers to deliver your strategy and what this requires in terms of product/services development and marketing.

S **kills:** The skills you will need to deliver your strategy and how you will acquire these skills.

T **echnology:** What technology you will need to deliver your strategy and how you will deliver this technology.

The most critical analysis you are using COST for is to identify gaps from where you are today and ensure your are addressing these gaps when you write your detailed D_5elivery Plan. In particular, it is all too easy to miss enablers that are not that significant for one specific choice but which are crucial to the overall success of the strategy. By using COST to look at enablers at an overall level we seek to avoid this.

I use a second acronym **ADAPT** to remember the topics of the latter sub-questions:

Align: The way in which the work to be done aligns into workstreams and how alignment can be achieved between this the organization's existing budgets and plan.

Delivery Office: What governance you will put in place and whether this includes a Delivery Office and if so, it's role and responsibilities.

Adjust: What needs to be tweaked and changed to better implement the strategy. This is iterative and based on learnings from the pilot.

Pilot: How you will test aspects of the strategy to determine how best to deliver it in full.

Track: How you will best track progress and use these findings to identify adjustments you need to make.

The two acronyms can also be used in the D_5elivery Information Table as per below:

D_5ELIVERY INFORMATION TABLE	1.	2.	3.	4.	5.	Overall
Customer			Add comments			
Offering			Add comments			
Skills			Add comments			
Technology			Add comments			

D₅ELIVERY INFORMATION TABLE	1.	2.	3.	4.	5.	Overall
Align		List workstreams				
Delivery Office		Add comments				
Adjust		Add comments				
Pilot		Add comments				
Track		Add comments				

Let's look the components of the two acronyms in turn, starting with Customers.

HOW YOU WILL REACH AND SERVE YOUR CUSTOMERS

What does your strategy imply about how you will reach your customers? How will you reach new customers? Will you build new skills organically or will you look to acquire an organization with these skills?

What about how you serve your existing customers? Will this stay the same or change? What does this imply about skills required?

For ITC's strategy to succeed, new customers need to be reached in the US, Canada, the UK and Germany. In the US this will include new customers who are smaller than existing customers. Outside the US, there needs to be a drastic increase in capacity. In addition, the sales teams in all countries need to understand the new modularized services offering so they can sell it.

Without reviewing what customers need as a specific enabler, it would be too easy to see the need for new sales skills and capacity in Canada, the UK and Germany, but to miss the important changes that are also required to support growth in the US.

HOW YOU WILL CHANGE YOUR OFFERING

What design and/or marketing work is required to develop your product and/or services offerings? Do you need extensive design and testing or it is more tweaking what we have and better packaging it? What are the implications for the product/services design teams? Do you have the right skills and sufficient capacity?

For ITC, there is limited design work required since the modularized services work is more in the line of repackaging than redesigning. Had we chosen recycling services too, then our answer would have been quite different here, with significant design work required.

WHAT SKILLS YOU REQUIRE

Are there new skills you require, or skills you have but will need in a more diverse set of locations? To what extent can you upskill existing staff? If you need to hire new staff, what skills will they need and where might you find these new staff? Are there any skills you need where you already know there is a shortage?

ITC needs new skills outside the US and also skills in the US to either build the webshop or the skills to manage an external supplier building it (as it definitely can't just be delegated and fingers crossed). Given the focus on renewals and new contracts in the US, we also need to ensure a robust and very effective business development process and possibly additional staff and expertise to drive success in this area.

WHAT TECHNOLOGY YOU REQUIRE

What technology is critical to success of your strategy? What could push it forward significantly? What, if you did not have it, would completely impede success?

For ITC, we know the webshop is critical in its own right but also crucial to enable the success of modularized services. Get the webshop wrong and ITC's strategy will fail. Knowing that the majority of technology projects fail for organizations of all sizes, significant focus needs to be put here to avoid failure.

ALIGNING INTO WORKSTREAMS

Now we have completed the COST acronym we can create a D_5elivery Plan. Begin by dividing the work to be done into workstreams. Each key choice—ITC has five of these—should form its own workstream. Now consider what other areas warrant their own workstream. For example, in any strategy HR and IT are typically required across more than one workstream and so it makes sense for these to be their own workstreams.

All D_5elivery Plans should include workstreams on governance and communications. The governance workstream should include the process, metrics, meetings and committees that will be used to share results of pilots (good and bad), facilitate best practice, review performance and support revisions to plans. It also needs to facilitate a can-do culture for delivering the strategy. The communications workstream should identify the different audiences to communicate with, the frequency and the type of messages. This workstream will need to be updated as you learn more, and as circumstances and needs evolve. A thought-through plan at the outset will provide a solid foundation on which to respond flexibly and nimbly.

Details should be provided on every workstream, including how each will be delivered and the milestones for the next quarter. This is also the time to decide on the workstream owners. Particularly for large workstreams, seek to have owners with their time fully dedicated to the workstream. Often a different mentality is required to deliver a new initiative versus "business as usual". Evidence suggests that where people have responsibility for both "business as usual" and for a new workstream, the new workstream will hardly ever happen as it is just too easy for the owner to be pulled into the "urgency" of their day-to-day responsibilities.

Overleaf is a D_5eliver Workstream Table—which is the start for the D_5elivery Plan for ITC:

D₅ELIVERY WORKSTREAMS TABLE			
	Workstream	Owner	Role
1	**Key accounts:** Grow the top six accounts not up for renewal before 2019	Raghu Jain	Head of Large Business
2	**Renewals:** win and increase base	Raghu Jain	Head of Large Business
3	**Modularized services:** drawn from packaged services and providing flexible à la carte services	Lisa Evereau	Head of Services
4	**Webshop:** which is easy to navigate and use	Des. Evans	Head of Product
5	**Overseas sales teams:** in Canada, Germany, UK, targeting existing customers with operations there		
6	**New contracts:** win three new contracts of at least $75m in the next three years, $2m profit per year	Janet Daley	Account Director
7	**IT:** to support IT requirements for initiatives; to ensure IT plans are aligned with strategy	Shelly Jonah	IT Director
8	**Finance:** ensure budget plans aligned with strategy; support as required	Irene Andrews	Financial Controller
9	**HR:** support recruitment of staff, especially for overseas sales initiatives; drive updating of staff's objectives to align with strategy	Jerome Delay	HR Director
10	**Marketing:** support development of material and pricing for modularized services, design of webshop and design of marketing collateral for overseas teams	Simon Burrows	Marketing Director
11	**Governance:** Create mechanisms and procedures to share learnings and best practices and monitor performance	James Edwards	Delivery Director
12	**Communication:** develop ongoing approach and facilitate deliver	Tim Hardy	Comms Director

Links to workstreams	Comments
	Will need to delegate targets to account directors; supported by Saffron Jones who was part of strategy design team
	Will need to delegate to account directors; supported by Saffron, part of design team
10. Marketing	Services Design Director will have heavy day-to-day involvement
7. IT & 10. Marketing	Will need close liaison with IT Director, who owns IT workstream
9. HR & 10. Marketing	Janet to be moved off Kirkton and Jameson and aligned full-time to overseas sales initiative
	Can build on existing work in business development
4. Webshop	Will need to work in partnership with Head of Product Business to deliver webshop
5. Overseas sales teams	
3. Modularized services, 4. Webshop & 5. Overseas sales teams	Newly created role, James promoted into this from commercial manager and was part of design team

ALIGNING WITH EXISTING BUDGETS AND PLANS

As you develop your D$_5$elivery Plan, replete with information on each workstream, including finances and technology requirements, consideration should be given to aligning this information with your organization's existing budgets and plans. The implications of the D$_5$elivery Plan should also be translated into what his means for individuals' objectives:

- **Alignment with budget:** With your strategy and its expected financial impact and required investment agreed, you want to make sure that all this is reflected in the budget. According to Strategic Planning Toolkit for Dummies,[29] 60% of organizations do not link their strategy to budget. Check that yours does, and if it does not, detail what needs to happen to address this, including what new revenue and cost lines need to be added and what needs to be removed as no longer part of the strategy. Reissue as soon as strategy is finalized and certainly within a matter of weeks.
- **Alignment of IT/other plans:** Ensure any IT development or other requirements for strategy are appropriately prioritized in plans.
- **Alignment of objectives:** Make any changes to objectives and bonus criteria of the division, of teams and individuals, to bring these into alignment with the strategy. Once you have the initiative owner in place, each needs to review the objectives of their team/the people they are working with to ensure they reflect the strategy. All business unit heads also need to review the objectives of all their staff to, firstly, make sure that other initiatives that are not part of strategy are not included (and if they are remove them) and, secondly, where appropriate, add new objectives related to the strategy.

DELIVERY OFFICE—YES, NO AND HOW TO

The Delivery Office—should you have one—presides over the governance of the program. It acts as the lynchpin coordinating across workstreams and can provide an adjudication role in the instance of disputes.

You may also choose to have a delivery person or team who get quite actively involved in the details of the workstream plans and in shaping these over time.

There are pros and cons to a Delivery Office with a more interventionist approach. It can add intellectual weight and rigor behind the D_5elivery Plan and where Delivery Office and workstream owners work well together, this will strengthen the plan and lead to more effective joint resolution of problems.

However, it will not work well if there is conflict between the Delivery Office and workstream owners, especially about who is really in charge (the workstream owner) or if the workstream owner does not take responsibility for their workstream and expects the Delivery Office to do all the work.

All this suggests that anyone in the Delivery Office needs to be respected, get on well with people, hold their ground when needed and also be willing to compromise.

Whatever you decide works best for your organization, if you have a Delivery Office, be sure to clearly define its role and remit and the responsibilities and decision rights of its team.

ADJUSTING YOUR APPROACH

No implementation plan will get everything 100% right from the outset so you need to be able to test approaches and adapt plans in light of your learnings.

Fast forward six months and take an example for ITC:

- **Workstream 3: Modularized services.** Suppose that there are quite different ways to modularize the services, with differing features and therefore different prices. Consider whether you can mock up collateral for the different options and test them with customers. Perhaps none of the options you test will turn-out to be optimal but a mix of them will. Some may not work well at all. These are all valuable insights that help potentially prevent committing more time and money to something that would fail.

You can never predict everything, so stay nimble and open and for each workstream think through the key things you could adjust, just like a scientist in a lab.

PILOTING YOUR APPROACH

Once you are open to being nimble, piloting is an easy follow-on. Essentially, it is about mindset. It's about having flexibility to test things and having a safe environment to share what doesn't work as much as what did. It is also knowing when to stop something when it is not working or being able to identify which parts are working and which are not, so you can improve output by focusing on what works.

Adjusting and piloting go together along with our final item tracking. They form an iterative loop that allow you to refine your approach until it is sufficiently honed to deliver your strategy.

Let's fast forward again with a couple of examples for ITC:

- **Workstream 4: Webshop.** Suppose that a first version of the webshop has been created. This would be a good time to do some user testing to identify any glitches or areas that are difficult to understand and navigate. Watching the customers use the webshop will provide lots of learnings and inform revisions that may otherwise have been missed.
- **Workstream 5: Overseas sales teams.** Suppose in Germany, ITC has been struggling for six months to recruit a head of the business and that despite getting lots of applicants none of them have been suitable. Then the workstream owner could organize a brainstorm with colleagues, including HR and the Delivery Office, to identify the issue(s) and how to best address these. For example, do the job adverts inaccurately reflect the

skills required, is the salary offered too low, is the role not being advertised in the right place or are they simply expecting too much and being too picky, and so on. Once diagnosed, a mitigating action can be decided and acted upon.

I often get asked is whether you will need to update the strategy as a result of the piloting and subsequent findings. In general, the answer is no. Your piloting is much more about how to deliver rather than changing the overall strategy itself. In addition, having spent so much time thinking the strategy through, unless conditions dramatically change or it turns out that one of the key initiatives just doesn't work at all—in which case you would likely need a new one to replace it, using your starting point to review the choices you rejected—then I suggest not tampering with it at all.

TRACKING YOUR PROGRESS

You need to hold yourself to account for delivering the strategy.

The milestones will help you to see if you are on course, as will feedback from customers, staff and colleagues.

You will no doubt experience times that are challenging or where doubts may emerge. If you have strong relationships in the organization, then you can really use these to support you both on problem solving but also in terms of morale and motivation.

As Edison said when referring to genius, but which also works just as well for a strategy process, is that "it's 1% inspiration and 99% perspiration."[30]

D₅ELIVERY CHECKLIST

- You have a D₅elivery Plan, divided into workstreams.
- Each workstream has an owner who has overall responsibility for delivery.
- Each owner is clear on what he/she needs to deliver and feels empowered to do so.
- The D₅elivery Plan includes details and milestones for each initiative and what the initiatives together will deliver.
- The D₅elivery Plan describes the approach to governance including metrics and committees.
- The D₅elivery Plan includes an ongoing approach to communication of your strategy.

A FINAL NOTE

*"Begin at the beginning and go on
'till you come to the end:
then stop."*

Lewis Carroll, *Alice in Wonderland*

Congratulations! You have a strategy that is actionable, rigorous and that has been created collaboratively.

Designing A Strategy That Works has shown you how to articulate your goal, identify options to meet it and make choices to create an integrated strategy that will work. Learning the steps outlined in this book also has benefits far beyond the areas of strategy design and delivery. The techniques in each of the chapters are standalone—for example, the techniques on structuring thinking and on the Minto Pyramid Principle® can transform verbal and written communications, from a short email to a more formal presentation. Or take the ability to accurately frame a problem: with clear framing, how often could misunderstanding and heartache be avoided?

Write down in the space provided overleaf three actions you commit to taking over the next 30 days. For example, you may want to do a one day off-site delivery planning session, or perhaps you need to determine the governance structure for the delivery phase.

1.

_____

_____

_____

_____

2.

_____

_____

_____

_____

3.

_____

_____

_____

_____

Take every opportunity to use and practice the techniques in this book. If you do so, a successful strategy is only the beginning of ever more success.

I would be delighted to hear from you with your feedback on your experience using techniques in this book. So please do get in touch with your comments at sarahthrift@insightconsults.com.

May your strategy be realized and every success yours.

APPENDIX

Commentary and answers to exercises in the book.

CHAPTER 1.1:

EXERCISE: IDENTIFYING SMART ONE QUESTIONS

Below is the completed table followed by commentary:

Answer Yes / No	S	M	A	R	T	O	N	E
1. What makes ITC profitable?	Y	N	N	Y	N	Y	Y	Y
2. Can ITC double its business?	N	Y	N	Y	N	N	Y	Y
3. What organizational changes are required for ITC to deliver $50m profit?	Y	Y	Y	N	N	Y	N	Y
4. What actions can ITC best take to achieve sustainable profit of at least $50m per year from 2018?	Y	Y	Y	Y	Y	Y	Y	Y
5. Create a proposition to generate significant and sustainable return for ITC and the customer	Y	Y	Y	Y	N	N	Y	N
6. How can ITC add 50% to its revenue in the next two years, while at least maintaining current profit margins?	Y	Y	Y	Y	Y	Y	Y	N

Comments:

1. What makes ITC profitable?
   - This will provide an answer that is quite narrow—almost like a yes/no question—and also one that refers to profitability today. This is not necessarily an indicator of profitability in the future and hardly the basis for a robust strategy.

2. Can ITC double its business?
   - Closed question (yes/no answer) without revealing the reasoning behind the answer and if yes, the actions that could be taken to deliver it. Also, doubling the business is vague. It is most likely to be inferred as doubling revenue, but with no mention of profit margins we have no idea whether it would yield the CEO's desired $50m profit (from today's $35m is 43% growth)

3. What organizational changes are required for ITC to deliver $50m profit?
   - Assumptive question. Unless a lot of prior work has already been done and has clearly revealed that organizational changes are what is needed, starting off with this question makes it likely you will fail to notice other solutions that would have much greater impact. Whenever I am contacted to help with determining organizational changes, a red flag immediately pops up in my head: organizational changes are very disruptive. This does not mean of course that they should never be undertaken, however they need to emerge as part of a broader strategy and not as the strategy itself.

4. What actions can ITC best take to achieve sustainable profit of at least $50m per year from 2018?
   - This is the most suitable question so far. It checks all the boxes for being a SMART ONE question. It takes the CEO's $50m profit goal as its own. This feels appropriate and not unrealistic—and so have given it a Y for relevant above—but this should be confirmed with stakeholders. It also does not narrow things down prematurely which could inadvertently limit solutions.

5. Create a proposition to generate significant and sustainable return for ITC and the customer
   - Stating the obvious, but this is not a question.

6. How can ITC add 50% to its revenue in the next two years, while at least maintaining current profit margins?
   - This question is clear and specific, but is it non-assumptive and also sufficiently expansive? Is the 50% target okay or assumptive. We would need to talk to stakeholders to be sure. In terms of being sufficiently expansive, is two years a sufficient timeframe? As a general rule, three years is the most common timeframe for a strategy. Beyond that, and certainly beyond five years really is too uncertain to design for with any precision. Two years, by contrast, can be a bit short-term in focus.

CHAPTER 2.1:

CONFIRMATION BIAS

Question demonstrating: What You See Is All There Is (WYIATSI):

Answer: Many people answer that the bat is $1. If this is the case, the ball must be $0.10 and so the bat is only $0.90 more than the ball. The correct answer is bat $1.05 and ball $0.05.

OVERCONFIDENCE BIAS

To estimate, all for 2015	Actual
1. GDP per capita in the US	$54,577
2. Proportion of books sold in electronic format in the US	20%
3. Proportion of American public school students qualifying for free or reduced school lunches	51%
4. Population of European Union	508m
5. Number of nations in the United Nations	193
6. Your organization's worldwide revenue 2015	For you to check (and not simply guess)
7. Your organization's worldwide net assets, 31 December 2015	For you to check (and not simply guess)
8. Your organization's worldwide employee turnover 2015 (%)	For you to check (and not simply guess)

CHAPTER 3.1:

SPECIFIC, MEANINGFUL AND TESTABLE HYPOTHESES

Below are comments on the example hypotheses in chapter 3.1:

- Our customers can be segmented.
  - This is neither specific nor meaningful. Pretty much all sets of customers can be segmented. The important point—which is not in the question—is how they can be segmented and what insight would this provide if you were to do so.
- We should focus on customers who are looking for a low cost offering to improve their profitability.
  - This is meaningful and testable, and somewhat specific, as it tells us where to focus. I would also want to know with this hypothesis or any similar ones, what this low cost offering would be.
- Our primary customer base needs a high-quality, efficient service and is prepared to pay a premium for this.
  - This is specific, meaningful and testable. You would need to talk to customers to test it, but it is specific enough to check there is a need for this.
- Revenue growth is important to restore ITC's profitability.
  - This is easily testable, but falls short in terms of being meaningful and specific. For example, I'd like to know how important revenue is to meeting the $50m profit target. For example is it 90% of the answer or 50%?—"important" in this context could mean either.

REFERENCES

INTRODUCTION:
1. Research conducted by William Schiemann as published in *Performance Management: Putting Research Into Action.*
2. Economist Intelligence Unit, *Why Good Strategies Fail: Lessons From The C-Suite,* July 2013.

FUNDAMENTALS:
3. Michael Porter quote, as published in *Harvard Business Review: What Is Strategy?,* November – December 1996.
4. You can read more about alignment vs. agreement on the Trium Group website www.triumgroup.com/organizational-trust-the-secret-ingredient-to-high-performing-organizations-2 or in the article by Ilan Mochari, *What's The Difference Between Agreement And Alignment?* www.inc.com/the-build-network/agreement-vs-alignment.html
5. In instances where there is very significant risk, then you may need to seek agreement as this engenders greater trust. For most strategy work, alignment is sufficient. You can read more at: Ryan McKeever, *How Aligned Is Your Organization?* Huffington Post, www.huffingtonpost.com/ryan-mckeever/how-aligned-is-your-organ_b_3881979.html
6. In chapter 5.2 an introduction to step D_5eliver is provided, but it does not cover this in-depth; to do so would require another book.

CHAPTER 1.1:
7. Covey, Stephen, R. (2004), *7 Habits Of Highly Effective People,* New York: Simon & Schuster.
8. Sessions, R. (1950), *New York Times: How A 'Difficult' Composer Gets That Way,* pg 89.
9. In the question, we have included the clause "to develop capabilities". You could write the question without this clause, as developing capabilities is likely to be an implicit need if a sustainable profit of at least $50m per year is required. I include it as it helps ensure specific focus on capabilities.

319

CHAPTER 2.1:

10. I am immensely grateful to Professor Jennifer Lerner and the team that put together and taught the incredibly powerful Leadership Decision Making program at Harvard Kennedy School. I was lucky enough to be a participant in June 2015 and appreciate all the ways in which their teachings opened my eyes to cognitive biases and their insidious effect on decision-making.

11. A film called *Moneyball* starring Brad Pitt and Jonah Hill based on the book *Moneyball: The Art Of Winning An Unfair Game* by Michael Lewis was released in 2011. I am grateful to Professor Lerner of the Harvard Kennedy School for introducing me to this film and book as part of the Leadership Decision Making program I attended.

12. Kahneman, D; Slovic, P; Tversky, A. (1982), *Judgment Under Uncertainty: Heuristics And Biases*, Cambridge: Cambridge University Press.

13. Office of National Statistics, *Causes of Death*, www.ons.gov.uk/peoplepopulationandcommunity/healthandsocialcare/causesofdeath

14. Centers for Disease Control and Prevention (CDC), *10 Leading Causes of Death* by Age Group, www.cdc.gov/injury/images/lc-charts/leading_causes_of_death_age_group_2014_1050w760h.gif

15. Saunders, B. (2012), "Opt-out Organ Donation Without Presumptions" *Journal of Medical Ethics*, Vol. 38: 69-72.

16. Kahneman, D. (2013), *Thinking Fast And Slow*, New York: Farrar, Straus and Giroux.

17. This exercise is adapted from the quiz in *The Power of Noticing: What The Best Leaders See*, by Professor Max H. Bazerman, who I was lucky enough to have as one of my professors on the Leadership Decision Making Program at the Harvard Kennedy School.

18. McKenzie, C.R.M., Liersch, M. J., & Yaniv, I (2008). "Overconfidence In Interval Estimates: What Does Expertise Buy You?" in *Organizational Behavior And Human Decision Processes*, Vol. 107, pg 179—91.

19. Alpert, Marc; Raiffa, Howard (1982), "A Progress Report On The Training Of Probability Assessors", chapter 21 in *Judgment Under Uncertainty: Heuristics And Biases*, edited by Daniel Kahneman, Paul Slovic, and Amos Tversky.
20. The investor of SWOT is disputed. Some say American management consultant Albert S. Humphrey devised the SWOT analysis technique while working for the Stanford Research Institute.
21. PESTLE and PEST are thought to have been invented by Harvard professor Francis Aguilar. He included a scanning tool called ETPS in his 1967 book, *Scanning the Business Environment*. The name was later tweaked to create the current acronym.
22. You may also see a PEST analysis talked about. This is the same concept, less the Legal and Environmental components.
23. Since this book was originally written, the UK has voted to leave the EU. This validates that using PESTLE for the UK was a good idea—and we have chosen to leave this showing the pre-Brexit situation.
24. Minto, B. (2002), *The Pyramid Principle*, Harlow, Essex: Pearson.
25. It is no coincidence that the pyramid, turned by 90 degrees, looks just like the question tree earlier. The same general principle applies; a governing thought or question supported by logically grouped findings or sub-questions. However, the pyramid can be, but does not need to be MECE—one fact, a change in regulation for example, can support a number of ideas higher up in the pyramid or later when we use the pyramid to structure our choices, which by definition are not collectively exhaustive.
26. We use "evidence" not "information" since we are testing our hypotheses with more than straight facts but with a range of evidence.

CHAPTER 5.1:
27. These first four enablers are part of the McKinsey 7S, which also includes strategy, style and shared values.

28. With thanks to Humphrey Walters, who I first leant this from when I attended his training in 2003.

CHAPTER 5.2:

29. Olsen, E. (2012), *Strategic Planning For Dummies*®, 2nd Edition, Hoboken, New Jersey: John Wiley & Sons, Inc.
30. Spoken statement (c. 1903); published in *Harper's Monthly* (September 1932)

BIBLIOGRAPHY

Banaji, M.R. & Greenwald, A.G. (2013), *Blindspot: Hidden Biases Of Good People*, New York: Random House.

Bazerman, M.H. (2014), *The Power Of Noticing*, 1st Edition, New York: Simon & Schuster.

Collins, T. (2009), *Change by Design*, New York: Harper Collins.

Friga, P.N. (2009), *The McKinsey Engagement*, New York: McGraw-Hill.

Covey, Stephen, R. (2013), *7 Habits Of Highly Effective People*, New York: Simon & Schuster.

Gelb, M.J. (1998), *How To Think Like Leonardo Da Vinci*, New York: Random House.

Gino, F. (2013), *Sidetracked: Why Our Decisions Get Derailed And How We Can Stick To The Plan*, Boston: Harvard Business School Publishing.

Heath, C. & Heath, D. (2013), *Decisive: How To Make Better Choices In Life And Work*, New York: Crown Publishing Group.

Kahneman, D. (2013), *Thinking Fast And Slow*, New York: Farrar, Straus and Giroux.

Kahneman, D., Slovic & P. & Tversky, A. (1982), *Judgment Under Uncertainty: Heuristics And Biases*, Cambridge: Cambridge University Press.

Kourdi, J. (2015), *Business Strategy: A Guide To Effective Decision-making*, 3rd Edition, London: The Economist in association with Profile Books Ltd.

McKenzie, C.R.M., Liersch, M. J. & Yaniv, I. (2008), "Overconfidence In Interval Estimates: What Does Expertise Buy You?" in *Organizational Behavior and Human Decision Processes*, Vol. 107.

Minto, B. (2002), *The Pyramid Principle*, Harlow, Essex: Pearson.

Montgomery, C. A. (2012), *The Strategist: Be the Leader Your Business Needs*, 1st Edition, New York: HarperCollins

Olsen, E. (2012), *Strategic Planning For Dummies®*, 2nd Edition, Hoboken, New Jersey: John Wiley & Sons, Inc.

Raisel, E.M. (1998), *The McKinsey Way*, New York: McGraw-Hill.

Raisel, E.M., & Friga, P.N. (2001), *The McKinsey Mind*, New York: McGraw-Hill.

Rosser, B. (2009), *Better, Stronger, Faster: Build It, Scale It, Flog It: The Entrepreneur's Guide To Success In Business*, Oxford, Infinite Ideas Limited.

Rumelt, R. (2011), *Good Strategy Bad Strategy: The Difference And Why It Matters*, London: Profile Books Ltd.

ACKNOWLEDGMENTS

The author would like to thank the following people for their support and contributions in making this book happen:

Irian Christine Weber, who has been an invaluable support to me as a friend and colleague since 2007. I am not quite sure where to start with the thanks... editor extraordinaire, thinking partner, problem solver, late night and early morning ear, and much more. Neither my business nor my book would be what it is without her.

Steve Hamilton for being a sounding board for many ideas in this book, for his sharp proofreading, editing, for mastering InDesign and laying out this third edition, and for putting up with my many late nights.

Paolo Cuomo for his support and his feedback following detailed readings of the book.

Tjaša Žurga Žabkar, founder of TJASART who created the cover illustration and all illustrations throughout the book.

AnneMarie Ward who skillfully and elegantly created the cover layout for this third edition.

Nishad Shamnadh for all his work to layout out the second edition of this book.

Tanicia Baynes, founder of Lollifox Design Studio, who laid out and designed the cover of the first edition of this book.

Professor Jennifer Lerner and the team that put together and taught the incredibly powerful Leadership Decision Making program at Harvard Kennedy School which opened my eyes to cognitive biases and their insidious effect on decision-making.

Dr David A. Bray for his mentorship which began at Harvard Kennedy School's Leadership Decision Making program and which continues to guide and inspire me.

Neil Almond, without whom none of this might ever have happened. He started it all, as I stood in his offices at a flip-chart, with the question: "If I could get a group of CEOs together, could you teach us what you do?"

Carolyn Kirkwood of Hunter Kirkwood Limited for her insights, expertise and mentorship and for inspiring the idea that strategy and structured thinking can be taught so effectively through a combination of workshops and coaching sessions.

Aliceson Robinson, a wonderful teacher, coach and workshop leader from whom I have learned a lot through the strategy courses we taught together.

Raj Modi, of www.strategyexpert.com who encouraged my writings and gave me invaluable feedback as a course participant.

Amy Celento who made herself, her home and her kitchen table available for me to write the first edition of this book.

My friend Katerina Zographos for her support and wisdom.

My friend Tracey Stanton for her care and encouragement.

My friends, colleagues and clients from McKinsey & Company who taught me so much and set high expectations for me to always aim for.

All the members of the Insight team over the years for their support and feedback that helped evolve the business and its services.

My clients and course participants—I have so enjoyed working alongside you, teaching you and learning with you.

And to Dr. Mohan Kataria, who is sadly no longer with us, but whose love and inspiration I will treasure forever.

INDEX

ABOUT INSIGHT CONSULTANCY SOLUTIONS

Insight Consultancy Solutions is a boutique consultancy and training company founded in 2007, with offices in the US and UK.

Insight delivers projects in strategy design, development and implementation, and provides expertise in multiple sectors including technology, financial services, education, public policy and NGOs.

A specialty of Insight is the design and facilitation of strategic problem-solving and communication courses for organizations, entrepreneurs and consultants. These courses are led by Sarah Thrift and her team of highly experienced consultants, who have spent thousands of hours using these tools and techniques in their own consulting work, in addition to the hundreds of hours they have spent teaching the material.

ABOUT THE AUTHOR

Sarah Thrift has 17 years experience working with businesses and nonprofit organizations on strategy, leadership and change management.

Prior to founding Insight Consultancy Solutions, Sarah worked at McKinsey & Company and as a policy advisor on business at the UK Treasury led by Gordon Brown, UK Chancellor and subsequently Prime Minister.

Sarah's mission is to pass her expertise and knowledge on strategic thinking, problem solving and decision-making to her clients. She teaches highly sought-after courses in these areas and shares the essence of her skills with those she cannot work with directly through her writing.

Sarah has a Masters in mathematics from Imperial College, London where she received the Governors' prize for achieving the top first class honors of her class. She has a great love of learning and has completed many courses since, including at Oxford University and Harvard University.